The
Mother's Day
Companion

By
Martin H. Rots

Table of Contents

Introduction

Everyone has a mother unless, of course, you were cloned. I'm not sure how that fits in, but I'm certain that topic is for a different book. This book is about mothers and their offspring...the good and the bad. Remember, Mother Theresa had a mother, but so did Charlie Manson.

The good mothers are truly inspirational in their unconditional love and support of their offspring. They willingly make sacrifices and if they're caused to suffer, they bear the pain quietly. They don't give up when it comes to their children. It doesn't matter if they've gotten a bad report card or have been abducted by aliens.

The bad mothers are an object lesson on things gone wrong, lack of real control in one's life and the ultimate consequences of failure. Some mothers are worse than others. It's one thing to neglect to teach your children good manners, it's quite another to drown them in a lake.

You never know which way things are going to go with your kids. Sometimes, bad mothering has been overcome with spectacular results.

Usually not though.

Unless your occasional motherly faux pas is abusive, go easy on yourself. Mothers are human, too. If you've ever had a guilty moment and thought to yourself, "Well, I wasn't really acting like a good mother there," reading about the really bad mothers will make you feel better. One thing you can always count on in life is that things could always be worse.

Count your blessings.

Initially, Mother's Day was conceived as a means of reconciliation after the American Civil War by a woman named Ann Jarvis in 1868. She initially called it "Mother's Friendship Day." In 1872, Juliet Ward Howe organized the first Mother's Day observance in New York City. It spread to Boston, but the initial enthusiasm for the event faded and it was forgotten by 1885.

The idea was revived in the early twentieth century by Ann Jarvis' daughter, Anna, and it evolved into a holiday to honor mothers who had lost a son serving our country. Eventually, the concept of Mother's Day was broadened to include all mothers. We honor American mothers each year on the second Sunday in May which was designated Mother's Day by Congress on May 6, 1914. Three days later, President Wilson signed the proclamation making it law, and we have honored American mothers each May since 1914.

Anna Jarvis started the tradition of wearing a white carnation on Mother's Day in honor of your mother. The florists knew a good thing when they saw it and began a marketing campaign to promote the wearing of a red carnation if your mother were alive and a white one if she had passed away. Chocolatiers helped promote Mother's Day with as much enthusiasm as the florists. It was the greatest financial opportunity for either group since the commercialization of Valentine's Day.

This book is divided into three sections. The first is quite serious and is about real mothers. Some, like Queen Victoria, were extraordinary mothers and are historical characters. Some of the mothers, like Rose Kennedy are from the recent past, others like Angelina Jolie are contemporary.

The section on Television Mom's covers the epitome of traditional American motherhood as portrayed on television in the 1950s. Squeaky clean characters like Harriet Nelson and June Cleaver joined us in our living rooms and projected a wholesome image. By the eighties, we had progressed to the grit of *Roseanne* and the outspokenness of *Murphy Brown*.

Movie Mothers covers some unique women on film. The most obvious of course is Mommy Dearest, Joan Crawford. Sophie made a choice no woman should have to make. Norman Bates' mother sat up in her room overlooking the Bates Motel.

Or did she?

Mothers play a unique role in our lives. Love them or hate them, there's no escaping our mothers. Even those who never knew their birth mother carry a fantasy image of what she must have been like, how she looked, how she smelled. Our childhood relationships with our mothers help form our personalities and establish the traits that define us as adults. On the battlefield, dying men call out to their mothers, their last hope, the woman who could always make it right...except for this time.

For most of us, she was that special woman who dried our tears and patched us up when we fell. She was our first teacher, patient and gentle, who applauded our accomplishments and smoothed over our failures. As adults, our relationships changed. After spending our teen years in rebellion, convinced our mothers were simpletons, we are astounded to find such a fountain of wisdom so close at hand.

I am presenting you, the reader, the following essays, anecdotes and stories of some famous and not so famous mothers. Some are outstanding examples, others... well, not so hot.

In spite of all the variables, it is amazing how many people succeed in life in spite of a less than idyllic childhood. Others, in spite of a strong maternal presence defy logic to become serial killers. Most of us fall somewhere in between.

Go figure.

Real Mothers

There are more outstanding mothers in real life than there are in the movies and television. Even though those movie and TV moms influence our vision of the typical American family and mother, the reality of motherhood is obviously much more complex than depicted by Hollywood and not nearly as entertaining.

There are many mothers deserving mention in this book, but there is limited space. Most of the real mothers presented here are Americans with the exception of Queen Victoria of Great Britain and the record holders for births, none of which are American. Eve too, although there's no real evidence that she ever existed, I felt it was important to include the alleged mother of the entire human race to this collection. Eve was certainly a mother if nothing else.

There seems to be no end of intelligent, motivated women in American history. Some of these women are the mothers and wives of prominent American politicians like Abigail Adams, who as his closest confidant, influenced her husband's thinking during the birth of the American nation. She was also responsible for educating her son, future President John Quincy Adams.   Together with Barbara Bush, they are the only two women in history to be married to a president of the United States and also be the mother of a President.

Others like Elizabeth Cady Stanton fought for women's rights all their lives as has Hillary Clinton whose potential to become the first woman president was recognized while she was still in college. Rose Kennedy gave birth to a political dynasty.

Showbiz mothers like Angelina Jolie are almost as well known for her philanthropic efforts and adoptions as she is for her acclaimed acting career. Madonna, she of the pointed brass bra fame, became the celebrity mom of Lourdes much to the delight of the paparazzi. Sharon Osbourne interacted in a very public forum with her family on MTV's reality show *The Osbournes*.

Also included in this chapter is the story of Susan Smith who did the unthinkable, she murdered her two small boys by drowning them, strapped into their car seats in a South Carolina lake.

As if this wasn't enough, she then accused a black man of carjacking her with the children asleep in the back seat. The horror she perpetrated was quickly uncovered by the police.

One thing about prominent mothers is they are no slouches when it comes to having children. Many of them bore and raised more than five children while living under extraordinary circumstances such as the American Revolution or ruling the largest empire the world has ever seen.

We also have three women who are only known for their dubious achievements in setting motherhood records. One for the youngest mother, the oldest, and the woman who holds the all time record for giving birth to the most children. None of these records should inspire any jealousy or the desire to break them for a notation in the Guinness Book of World Records.

Obviously, there are certain records that are less desirable than others.

Sit back and enjoy these mothers who made their mark. Their roles in forming their children's and husband's lives are undeniable. Whether real or fictional, our world would be a much different place without these women.

Rose Kennedy
Mother of a Dynasty

Rose Fitzgerald Kennedy was Irish-American politician John "Honey Fitz" Fitzgerald's first born. She entered the world July 22, 1890 in Boston, Massachusetts and lived to be 104 years old. No one could have predicted the long, turbulent life the grand dame of Massachusetts, if not the United States itself, would lead. Her children would include a president, two U.S. senators and an Ambassador to Ireland. She outlived five of her nine children. Her life was one of triumph and tragedy, elation and sorrow.

Rose graduated from high school at sixteen, determined to continue her education at Wellesley. Her father had other plans for the girl and she soon found herself at Boston's Convent of the Sacred Heart. Rose and Honey Fitz toured Europe in 1908. Staunch Catholics, an audience at the Vatican with Pope Pius X was arranged for the two of them. Rose later studied French and German in the Netherlands before returning to Boston.

It wasn't long before she became reacquainted with young Joe Kennedy, the dapper, confident son of a Boston saloon owner she had met the year before. Rose was smart, pretty, and it didn't hurt that her father was the mayor of Boston. The young Kennedy already had political aspirations, but the mayor was not impressed and tried to dissuade his daughter from marrying Joe to no avail.

On October 7, 1914, she and Joseph Kennedy Sr. were married in Boston. It wasn't long before they started what would become a very distinguished family of nine children.

Their first child, Joseph Jr. was born on July 25, 1915 in Boston. Joe Sr. had political ambitions for his eldest son that would never be fulfilled. Contemplating a post-war political career, and envious of his younger brother Jack's heroic exploits in the Pacific theater of war, Joe Jr. volunteered to pilot a plane, overburdened with explosives, to a secret French target. He was killed on August 12, 1944 crossing the English Channel on the mission. The plane exploded under mysterious circumstances, and his body never found.

John Kennedy, the next born, fared better, surviving a collision between the PT boat he skippered and a Japanese destroyer in the south Pacific. Young Jack performed heroically to save his crew and the incident became part of his legend. He was elected to the House of Representatives in 1948 and the U.S. Senate in 1952. In November 1960 he was elected President of the United States but sadly, was assassinated three years later in November of 1963, never fulfilling his promise.

Born September 13, 1918, Rosemary Kennedy was destined to play another tragic role in the Kennedy saga. After a normal childhood, Rosemary began to have violent fits as a teenager. Afraid that any hint of mental illness in the family would squelch political ambitions for his eldest son, Joe Jr., Joe Sr. portrayed his eldest daughter as developmentally challenged, which he felt was more socially acceptable than mentally ill and bore less stigma. At 23, Rosemary was lobotomized in a Washington DC hospital in an effort to control her mood swings. The operation left her with the mind of a two year old and she spent the remainder of her life in various institutions. She passed away in 2005 at the age of 86 in a mental facility in Fort Atkinson, Wisconsin. Her siblings, Ted and Jean were at her bedside when she died.

Kathleen "Kick" Kennedy was born February 20, 1920 in Brookline, Massachusetts. She accompanied her father, Joe Sr., when he went to London in 1938 to represent the United States as Ambassador to the Court of Saint James. London agreed with Kick and it wasn't long before she was caught up in the swirl of London society. She met and married William Cavendish, Marquess of Hartington, a Protestant. Rose, a staunch Catholic, refused to attend the ceremony and encouraged other members of the family to do likewise. Her oldest brother, Joe Jr. was the only family member to attend the ceremony. Kick's husband was killed in action only a few months after their marriage. Kathleen died in a plane crash in France on May 13, 1948 at the age of twenty-eight.

Eunice Kennedy, the fifth of the Kennedy children, was born on July 10, 1921. She married Robert Sargent Shriver on May 23, 1953. Her second oldest child, Maria, married actor and California governor, Arnold Schwarzenegger. Eunice, her awareness increased by her sister Rosemary's condition, was instrumental in creating and promoting the Special Olympics. She passed away of natural causes on August 11, 2009 with her family at her bedside.

Patricia Kennedy, born May 6, 1924, managed to avoid the political limelight, preferring the world of motion pictures and Hollywood. Young and impressionable, she was influenced by Joe Kennedy Sr.'s stint as a producer in Los Angeles and worked in the motion picture business for several years. Patricia's other passion in life was travel and she acted as a foreign correspondent, sharing her adventures with American readers. On April 24, 1954, she married actor, Peter Lawford in New York City. The couple divorced in 1966 and she never remarried. Patricia passed away on September 17, 2006 at the age of 82 after a short battle with pneumonia.

Rose's second most prominent son, Robert F. Kennedy, was born on November 20, 1925. After years of private schools, Robert attended and graduated from Harvard University in March 1948 with a degree in government. Returning from an extended European tour, he attended the University of Virginia School of Law, graduating in June 1951. Robert entered politics and was appointed United States Attorney General by his brother, President John F. Kennedy in 1961. Robert was assassinated in Los Angeles at the Ambassador Hotel while campaigning for president on June 5, 1968.

Jean Kennedy, the youngest of the Kennedy sisters, was born on February 21, 1928. She was the only one of the sisters to take an active interest in politics. On May 19, 1958, she married Stephen Smith in New York's St. Patrick's Cathedral. She and her husband were present at the Ambassador Hotel in Los Angeles when her older brother, Bobby, was murdered by Sirhan Sirhan. In 1993, President Clinton appointed Jean as Ambassador to Ireland, a post she held until September 1998.

Today she has residences in both New York City and Washington D.C..

Edward (Ted) Kennedy, last of the generation to carry on the Kennedy family political tradition, was born on February 22, 1932. He entered politics in 1962 when he won a special election held to fill his brother John's vacant Senate seat. He was subsequently re-elected eight more times during the course of his political career. Tragedy once more raised its head when in 1969, he was involved in scandal. While giving Mary Joe Kopechne, a former campaign worker for his brother Bobby, a ride home from a party on Chappaquiddick Island, Massachusetts, Kennedy accidently drove off a bridge and into the water. He was able to escape but Mary Joe, drowned. Kennedy failed to report the late night accident until the following day precipitating a major scandal. He sought the Democratic presidential nomination in 1980 but was defeated by the incumbent, Jimmy Carter. Kennedy continued to support liberal democratic causes until his death from a brain tumor in August, 2009.

Rose Kennedy outlived four of her children. She was outspoken her entire life. She passed away on January 22, 1995 at the age of 104 from complications of pneumonia. Arguably, as a mother, no one contributed more to American government. The Kennedys were truly the first family of America and Rose, its mother.

The Record Holders
Youngest, Oldest, Most

There are records for motherhood. They keep records of everything and have been doing so forever. The British took an inventory of the kingdom in 1086 which resulted in the aptly named Doomsday Book and substantially higher taxes for everyone.

This record keeping obsession wasn't always a good thing for the average citizen.

Europeans were good at creating and maintaining records in spite of their endless wars throughout the centuries. Meticulous record keeping aside, who are the record holders for motherhood? Who had the most children? Who was the oldest or youngest to give birth? The answers are astounding.

We all remember growing up and there was one family that was bigger than all the others. They didn't have a family, it was more like a tribe or depending on the neighborhood, their own private gang no one could penetrate. The kids were always the skinniest kids in the neighborhood and they fought amongst themselves a lot. Everyone knew better than to interfere with their squabbles. If you did, they would all turn on you. When I asked my mother why they had so many kids, all she said was, "Catholic," and shrugged her shoulders. Her answer satisfied me for the time being. At seven, I didn't really understand the religious implications of sex any better than I do now.

When I think of big families, I think twelve, maybe fourteen kids. That's like a farm family from times past in rural America. I've known a few families like that and always marveled at them. At home it was just my brother and I. We had bunk beds once and shared a room for a short time, but I can't relate to dormitories. Most of the time I always had my own bedroom growing up.

According to The Guinness Book of World Records 2004 Edition, the record for live births is held by a woman from Shuya, Russia. Her name has been lost in the mists of history, but she was the first wife of one Feodor Vassilyev. I find it incredible that her husband's name was recorded as the father, but no one thought to jot down her name. By any stretch of the imagination, this was one incredible woman.

Feodor (evidently incapable of any kind of restraint) impregnated his wife twenty-seven times between 1725 and 1765 resulting in sixty-nine live births. All but two survived their first year of life. During that time, the poor woman allegedly gave birth to sixteen sets of twins, seven sets of triplets and four sets of quadruplets. Not a single birth among them and all this before fertility drugs.

I always thought that fourteen was a houseful.

The problem with this claim is that it's hard to prove. It's supposedly substantiated by church records, but those can be falsified. It seems improbable that a woman and almost all of her children survived considering the dangers of childbirth in that time and place. Obviously, there is no photographic evidence available from the eighteenth century.

If it is true, it's quite incredible.

The youngest mother in history is well documented including photographic evidence. When Lina Medina's parents brought their young daughter to the doctor in Lima, Peru in 1939, it was initially thought she had developed a large tumor. Much to everyone's amazement, subsequent x-rays revealed she was very pregnant. Lina's remaining pregnancy was carefully monitored and documented by Peruvian doctors.

She was five years old.

On May 14, 1939, little Lina gave birth to a six and one half pound, healthy baby boy by caesarean section. She named the baby Gerardo. He was healthy and initially raised as her brother by her parents. Gerardo didn't learn Lina's true identity until he was ten.

According to Lina's parents, Lina's body reached menarche at the age of two and a half and she had developed prominent breasts when she was four. Lina never revealed the circumstances of her pregnancy. Her father was arrested for rape and incest initially, but the police quickly ended the investigation declaring him innocent of any wrongdoing. The doctors speculated that she was so young, Lina may not have even realized when or how it happened. No one was ever arrested for the crime against the child.

Gerardo succumbed to cancer at the age of forty in 1979. Lina had another son with her husband in 1972 but little is known of him. In 2002 she was working as a secretary for Dr. Gerardo Lozada, the surgeon who delivered her son.

At the other end of the spectrum we find Omkari Panwar, 70 of Muzaffarnagan, India giving birth to twins on June 27, 2008 via cesarean section. The boy and girl weighed two pounds each and were healthy.

Her husband Charan, was seventy-seven and overjoyed to finally have a son. He made no comment on his new born daughter. The couple were determined to leave a male heir and Omkari became pregnant using the IVF method. It was a difficult pregnancy and the procedure cost them almost everything they had or could borrow from friends and relatives.

Mind you, they already have two adult daughters and grandchildren, but this is India. In the rural areas of India, it is still common to drown baby girls. They're seen as just another mouth to feed and dowry to pay. The whole concept of having a male heir is very important to Indian men. This is an ancient idea that unfortunately still persists today.

Omkari recovered from her surgery in her daughter's mud hut. It is unclear who will raise Charan and Omkari Panwar's new heirs, but they are exceedingly grateful for their infant son and hope to live to see him walk.

Madonna
Like a Virgin?

Madonna Louise Ciccone was born in Bay City, Michigan on August 16, 1958 to Silvio and Madonna Louise Ciccone. The family moved to the northern suburbs of Detroit soon after where Silvio found work as a design engineer in the automotive industry. Her mother died when she was five, stricken by breast cancer. Her father remarried and she grew up in what is now Rochester Hills, Michigan. Madonna went to Rochester Adams High School where she was almost as well known for her excellent grades as she was for her outlandish dress and behavior.

She received a dance scholarship to the University of Michigan and moved to Ann Arbor for the fall 1976 term. An instructor in the dance program encouraged her to go to New York and that was exactly what she did late in 1977. She arrived in Manhattan with thirty-five dollars and a suitcase. She didn't know a soul, but she was determined to make it in the Big Apple.

Madonna lived in extreme urban poverty and worked as a waitress while auditioning around town. She fronted punk bands and learned to sing. She became a regular on the Manhattan dance club circuit, known for her sense of fashion as much as for her dancing and singing.

In July 1983, she released her first album entitled simply, *Madonna*. The album rose to number eight on the Billboard Charts. It was her next album, *Like a Virgin* that made her a star when it reached the number one position. Not long after, she appeared with Rosanna Arquette in the film, *Desperately Seeking Susan* and married Hollywood bad boy, Sean Penn.

It was the beginning of the period when the good Catholic girl began to go out of her way to provoke the church with her use of religious imagery in her songs and especially her videos. The video for Like a Prayer provoked the Pope to condemn it and ban it from being viewed by Catholics.

A lot of them watched it anyhow.

She lost her contract to endorse Pepsi as a result of the controversy, but she got to keep all the money. She gave up Sean Penn in the midst of the turmoil, preferring her career to wedded bliss. It wasn't the end of her problems with the Pope either.

In 1990 she combined sex and religious imagery on the Blonde Ambition World Tour. Once again the Pope, who had been following her career closely on MTV, was disturbed by reports of the other Madonna masturbating on stage while singing *Like A Virgin*. Once again, the Vatican issued a statement condemning her and public masturbation. Other Catholic organizations jumped on the bandwagon calling for a boycott of the tour and public masturbation. It had no effect on her tour or reported incidents of public masturbation. It was all great publicity and Madonna was no one's fool. As a former Catholic school girl, she recognized the opportunity the Pope's condemnation created for her. The Vatican's actions had little effect other than publicizing the tour.

In November 1990 she released *Justify My Love* creating instant controversy. The video featured lesbian sex and sadomasochism. It was banned by everyone and went straight to number one in the U.S. charts. As P.T. Barnum was fond of saying, "No one ever went broke underestimating the good taste of the American public."

Madonna took it to the bank.

In the midst of all this she appeared nude in both Playboy and Penthouse and divorced Sean Penn after four years of wedded confusion. She quickly learned that publicity sells records. A nude coffee table book soon followed. It seemed Madonna was naked or almost naked everywhere you looked, usually with a crucifix and a wicked look painted across her face. She was not the kind of girl you took home to mother.

She had hairy armpits, too.

She spent the next five years upsetting everyone. When she came to Israel, Orthodox Jews protested her presence as unholy. She made the Puerto Rican's angry when she used their flag as a sex object at a concert in San Juan.

When David Letterman introduced her on his show, he said she'd, "slept with some of the biggest names in the entertainment industry," to get to the top. It was tongue in cheek, but Madonna walked out with an attitude. She let loose with a string of foul language and shoved a pair of her panties at the exasperated host.

When it seemed that Madonna couldn't possibly behave any wilder, she became pregnant by her personal trainer, Carlos Leon. On October 14, 1996, she gave birth to a healthy baby girl she named Lourdes Maria Ciccone Leon. Madonna quickly moved on and Lourdes father, Carlos, was soon forgotten after his fifteen minutes of fame.

In 1999, Madonna met English film director Guy Ritchie through mutual friends Sting and Trudy Styler in London. By the end of the year, Madonna was pregnant with Ritchie's baby. A son, Rocco, was born to them on August 11, 2000. The couple married on December 22, 2000 in Scotland.

At the 2003 MTV Video Music Awards, Madonna performed the tune *Hollywood* with Christine Aguilera and Brittany Spears. During the performance, she deep kissed both women, insuring a new round of publicity and controversy.

On January 15, 2005, Madonna performed John Lennon's *Imagine* for the Tsunami Aid fundraiser

In 2006, Madonna got the itch to be a mother again, not a real mother with stretch marks and real labor and all that, she decided to adopt. When the adoption agency got a load of her in the pointy brass bra playing with herself on stage, they must have thought, "Yep, she's the one."

In October 2006, Madonna began the process to adopt a Malawi orphan named David Banda Mwale. The adoption was contested and after a long legal battle that reached the Malawi supreme court was finalized on May 28, 2008. She was divorced from Guy Ritchie the same year.

In 2009 Madonna figured she was on a roll and returned to Malawi to adopt a little girl, Chifundo "Mercy" James. Once again, she faced legal hurdles. Fortunately, these were quickly resolved and the adoption was successfully completed in June.

Madonna is so much more than just a performer or even an artist. As a woman she succeeded in a notoriously tough business on her own terms. As a businesswoman, she has few equals. Her success was tremendous and she accomplished it using the power of publicity and shock tactics.

You have to admire her tenacity.

Hillary Rodham Clinton

Hillary Rodham Clinton was born on October 26, 1947, in Chicago, Illinois. Her father, Hugh Ellsworth Rodham was a conservative businessman and devotee of Barry Goldwater. Her mother, Dorothy Emma Howell, was a homemaker more inclined to liberal values.

A prodigy, Hillary was a classic over achiever in school. Well liked by students and teachers alike, she thrived in the environment. She attended public school where she excelled in both academics and athletics. She was a member of the National Honor Society and a National Merit finalist in 1965.

In 1962, she experienced a life-changing meeting with Martin Luther King in Chicago. She was selected by her Methodist youth counselor to accompany him to the meeting with the famed civil rights leader. It was to have a profound impact on how the bright, young woman was to think long into the future.

In spite of her parent's different political views, the one thing they agreed upon was that Hillary's future should not be limited by her gender. Even her conservative father knew that Hillary had a special gift. Her parents have always been tirelessly supportive of her endeavors.

In the fall of 1965, she started her freshman year at Wellesley College in Wellesley, Massachusetts. Majoring in political science, she joined the Young Republicans in her freshman year and was soon after elected president of the club. Her initial enthusiasm for the group waned as she became interested in the Civil Rights and Anti-War movements of the mid-sixties. In spite of all the rhetoric of the era, Hillary decided to work from within for change. She graduated with honors in 1965 with a Bachelor of Arts, majoring in political science.

After a summer spent exploring Alaska financed by odd jobs, she began Yale Law School. During her freshman year, she sat on the board of the Yale Law Review. As a sophomore, she worked with the Yale Child Study Center and the Yale-New Haven Hospital investigating cases of child abuse.

It was at Yale that she met fellow-student, Bill Clinton, in the spring of 1971. When she took a summer internship in Oakland, California, he followed her west for the summer. When he proposed marriage to her in 1973, Hillary passed in favor of beginning her career. Bill was persistent and continued his campaign. Hillary was equally stubborn about maintaining her own identity and consistently refused his proposals.

She worked in Washington D.C. as part of the staff investigating the Watergate scandal that eventually led to the resignation of Richard M. Nixon. In 1974 with her investigative work complete and after failing the bar exam in Washington D.C., Hillary went to Arkansas and Bill Clinton in spite of friends advising her to stay in Washington D.C..

Although she still refused to marry him, the two bought a modest house together in Fayetteville, Arkansas in 1975. Hillary finally agreed to marry Clinton and they were married in their Fayetteville home on October 11, 1975. Hillary decided to keep her maiden name for professional reasons which upset both families.

Bill Clinton didn't seem to care.

When he was elected Arkansas Attorney General in 1976, they relocated to Little Rock, and she joined the politically influential Rose Law Firm. In addition to her professional services, she continued her work for children's rights and in family law publishing several important papers on the subject.

In 1978, Bill was elected Governor of Arkansas and Hillary became Arkansas' First Lady. In 1979, Hillary was made a full partner of the Rose Law Firm, the first woman to achieve that status in the long history of the firm.

On February 27, 1980, Hillary gave birth to daughter, Chelsea, in Little Rock.
In November 1980, Bill was defeated for re-election as governor by Frank D. White. He regained the office two years later and retained it until his election as president in 1991.

During her husband's presidential campaign, the ever outspoken Hillary made some controversial remarks regarding Tammy Wynette's advice regarding men. She questioned women's traditional role at the end of the twentieth century in America. Rather than view her new position as potential First Lady of the United States as largely symbolic, she used her position as an opportunity to advance her own agenda. Bill Clinton stressed Hillary's experience, intellect and qualifications. He assured America that if elected, she would also bring her talents to the White House.

Hillary followed Bill to the White House as First Lady in 1992 and took an active role in his administration. The opposition referred to her and Clinton sarcastically as co-President or even "Billary" as a catch-all term for the two. Outwardly at least, Hillary was impervious to their taunts and sexist insults. As a team, the two were as effective in Washington D.C. as they had been in Little Rock, Arkansas.

In 1998, Bill was accused of engaging in sexual relations (in spite of his lame attempt to redefine what sexual relations consist of) with a White house intern named Monica Lewinsky. This wasn't the first time Bill had been accused of philandering. While Governor of Arkansas, he had been accused of conducting affairs with state employee, Paula Jones and singer Gennifer Flowers.

Hillary supported Bill through the entire congressional investigation and impeachment hearings although privately, she considered ending the marriage. She stayed with Clinton as America speculated why. She was admired for the way she handled the affair. It was good experience for her role later in life as Secretary of State, the top United States diplomat to the world.

When Clinton left office in 2001, Hillary was encouraged to run for the Congressional seat left vacant by the retirement of Senator Patrick Daniel Moynihan in New York. Upon leaving the White House, the Clintons relocated to Chappaqua, New York, north of Manhattan and began her successful campaign for the Senate seat. She was reelected to the seat again in 2007.

On January 20, 2007 Hillary announced her intention to run for President of the United States. Early in her campaign, Hillary was far and away, the front runner. Her momentum began to falter in January 2008 when she finished third to John Edwards and Barack Obama in the Iowa Democratic Caucus. A misinterpreted remark perceived to be a racial slight lost the support of the African-American community even though Obama himself declared that it shouldn't be interpreted as such. It wasn't long before Rodham's bid for the presidency was over. Reluctant to accept the office of Vice-President, Rodham became Secretary of State in the new Obama administration.

Rodham has been an advocate of children's rights for her entire career. In spite of the demands on her time, she has always been involved in the raising of Chelsea who has by all reports grown up to be an intelligent, fine young woman, just like her mother before her.

Abigail Adams
Barbara Bush
Presidential Wives and Mothers

Abigail Adams and Barbara Bush are unique among American women and mothers. They alone have been married to and given birth to an American president. Abigail was married to John Adams, one of the architects of the revolution and the second President of the United States. Her son John Quincy Adams was the sixth president. Barbara Bush is married to George Herbert Walker Bush, forty-first president and mother of George W. Bush, the forty-third.

Abigail Smith, born November 11, 1744, was just seventeen when John Adams began to court her. His friend, Richard Cranch was engaged to Abigail's older sister, Mary, and it was through Cranch that Adams came to know Abigail in 1762. In an era when women were seldom educated, Abigail usually had her nose buried in a book and he found that extremely attractive. Even though Adams had been acquainted with her since she was a child (they were third cousins), he was nine years her senior.

John and Abigail were married on October 25, 1764 by her father, the Reverend William Smith at the family home in Weymouth, Massachusetts. They moved into a farmhouse outside Braintree before moving to Boston where John's law practice began to thrive.

Abigail gave birth to six children while helping her husband give birth to a new nation. There were long separations in the beginning of the marriage and Abigail was left alone when her first two children, Abigail (known as Nabby) and John Quincy were small. John worked in Philadelphia for months while the Declaration of Independence was written, debated and finally signed on July 4, 1776.

During these absences, the two carried on a long correspondence. Adams turned to his wife as a trusted confidant and advisor. Their letters, of which there are many, are full of anguish and debate. Abigail proved to be an able counselor to John during the darkest days of the revolution and he often turned to her.

Abigail and her eldest son, future president John Quincy, watched the Battle of Bunker Hill from a hilltop near their home.

Abigail was the first First Lady to live in the White House, then known as the President's House. It was still under construction when she and John took occupancy and Washington D.C. was for the most part, a very large swamp. Abigail, in spite of her mighty intellect, was of frail health and the environment was hard on her, but she never complained. John was defeated for re-election by Thomas Jefferson in 1801 and the couple returned to Massachusetts.

Abigail was an early advocate for women's rights and in spite of her best efforts, she was for the most part ignored by the founding fathers. Both she and John were outspoken against the evils of slavery. Even though she was raised by a pastor, she rejected the conventional Christian trinity in favor of believing in one God.

When her eldest son John Quincy became involved in politics, Abigail played the familiar role of trusted advisor. He, like his father, had genuine respect for

Abigail's intellectual prowess. When he was elected as the sixth president in 1826, Abigail had already passed away. Abigail Quincy Adams, died on October 28, 1818, succumbing to typhoid fever. She predeceased her husband John by almost eight years.

Barbara Pierce Bush was born to Pauline and Marvin Pierce in Flushing, New York on June 8, 1925. She and Franklin Pierce (14th president of the United States) shared a common ancestor, Thomas Pierce. Her father, Marvin, worked as publishing executive in New York City.

As a girl, Barbara attended private schools and met her future husband, George Herbert Walker at a Christmas dance when she was sixteen years old. They began dating, but George's courtship was interrupted by WWII. With George gone piloting a torpedo bomber, Barbara waited for his return back in New York. When George returned home on leave for Christmas 1944, he asked Barbara to marry him. The two were married on January 6, 1945, two days shy of her twentieth birthday.

Her first born son, George Walker Bush, forty-third President of the United States was born July 6, 1946 in New Haven, Connecticut where his father, George Bush Senior was attending Yale. He and the rest of his siblings were raised in Midland and Houston, Texas. Barbara had two daughters, Pauline who died of leukemia at the age of three and Dorothy, the youngest of the children. George's next youngest brother, John aka "Jeb," served as the forty-third governor of Texas. Neil Bush gained notoriety during a messy 2003 divorce during which, he testified he had contracted Herpes from prostitutes in Bangkok and Hong Kong. Barbara's youngest son, Marvin has so far avoided the spotlight and notoriety.

Barbara launched her campaign for literacy in the United States when George served as Vice-President under Ronald Reagan. She continued her work when he was elected President in 1988 and founded the Barbara Bush Foundation for Family Literacy.

While Bush Senior was in office, Barbara took an interest in the White House Historical Association. She has also raised funds for the White House Endowment Fund which is charged with the historical restoration of the White House.

Since her husband left politics, she has continued with her literacy work by chairing the Barbara Bush Foundation for Family Literacy. She also serves on the Board of Directors of both the Mayo Clinic and Americares.

Elizabeth Cady Stanton
American Woman

Every woman in America should know the name Elizabeth Cady Stanton, unfortunately, most American women have never heard of her. In an era when equal rights for women is taken for granted or unappreciated by many women, her fight for the vote is almost forgotten. Women were not granted the right to vote until August 26, 1920 when Congress passed the Nineteenth Amendment. Stanton's tireless devotion was instrumental in achieving what was then known as "suffrage." She unfortunately, passed away in 1902 and didn't live to see the fruits of her labor.

Born Elizabeth Cady on November 12, 1815 in Johnstown, New York, Stanton was the eighth of eleven children born to Daniel and Margaret Cady Stanton. Her father was an attorney, judge and Congressman from 1814 until 1817.

Elizabeth's childhood was marred by the death of five of her siblings including all her brothers. Her mother was devastated by the loss of her children and retreated into depression. As Margaret Stanton withdrew, Elizabeth turned to her father. Elizabeth demonstrated an early interest in the law, which her father encouraged. It was this curiosity that led her to realize that women in the United States had virtually no rights. They were essentially the property of their husbands, unable to vote, own property or hold public office among other things.

Her father owned a slave named Peter Teabout and Elizabeth got a firsthand look at what was once called "that peculiar institution." Elizabeth enjoyed Peter's company and took him to church with her as a girl. Teabout was freed on July 4, 1827 when the state of New York abolished slavery.

Elizabeth was educated in a coed environment at the Johnstown Academy where she studied mathematics, Greek and Latin. Tutored in Greek by a neighbor, the Reverend Simon Hosack, she excelled in her study of the language and successfully competed with the boys in her class. Hosack encouraged her to continue with her education after graduating from

Johnstown Academy in 1830 and Elizabeth enrolled in the Troy Female Seminary.

Elizabeth became active in both the anti-slavery and temperance crusades as a young woman and it was during this time she met her future husband, Henry Stanton. Stanton worked the circuit, delivering fiery speeches condemning slavery and calling for the prohibition of alcohol. For the young Elizabeth, it was love at first site and the couple were married in 1840.

Elizabeth had a novel idea for the time. She instructed the pastor to drop the phrase, "promise to obey" from the wedding vows. Her new husband was not necessarily in agreement with her request. While Stanton worked tirelessly to free the slaves, he wasn't as enthusiastic about freeing women, black or white.

He was further concerned when she refused to be referred to as Mrs. Henry Stanton. In spite of their fundamental difference of opinion regarding women's suffrage, she and Henry were married until his death in 1887.

In 1840 while honeymooning in London, Elizabeth met feminist and abolitionist Lucretia Mott at the International Anti-Slavery Conference. When the female delegates to the convention were refused participation, a lifelong bond was formed between the two women. Together, they would found the fledgling American women's movement. The conference also marked the beginning of a long relationship with the great abolitionist orator, Frederick Douglas, who initially supported their cause.

Elizabeth gave birth to the first of her five sons in 1842. She named him Daniel Stanton after her father. Over the next fourteen years she gave birth to five more children, three sons and two daughters. In 1859, she gave birth to son Robert, her last borne, when she was forty four years of age.

How Elizabeth found time to do anything is beyond me.

At the time it was quite incredible for any woman to pursue interests outside the home. While busy raising her family, she founded what would become the women's movement. Elizabeth was one of the first women in American history who pursued lofty political goals while parenting at the same time.

In 1848, Elizabeth and Lucretia Mott organized the first Women's Rights convention held at Seneca Falls, New York. At the convention, Stanton read her Declaration of Sentiments. It paraphrased the Declaration of Independence by saying that "all men *and women* are created equal." This preposterous statement was followed by the equally preposterous notion that women should be granted the vote. It was a revolutionary idea in nineteenth century America.

Elizabeth wasn't asking though, she was demanding the vote.

Modest by today's standards, the convention was attended by less than four hundred women. The birth of the women's movement was followed soon after by another convention in Rochester, New York where Stanton spoke to an even bigger gathering of women. The movement, as expected, began to grow exponentially.

In 1851, she met Susan B. Anthony and the two initially joined forces in the temperance movement. It would be the beginning of a long and exhausting partnership that lasted the remainder of the women's lives. It wasn't long before they turned their attention back to the feminist cause.

At the conclusion of the American Civil War, Stanton and Anthony broke with the abolitionists who successfully pushed the Fourteenth and Fifteenth Amendments through Congress. The amendments gave former male slaves the right to vote but continued to deny the franchise to women. When the abolitionists refused to consider including it in the amendments, the women split with them to pursue their own interests.

It was at this time that the women broke with Frederick Douglas who dismissed the women's movement. He contended that white women had enough power via their husbands, they didn't need the vote. The women had worked tirelessly for years on behalf of the abolitionist movement and when their dream was within their grasp, the women were abandoned and their work discredited. It became shamefully ugly on both sides.

Over the next forty years, Stanton and Anthony worked tirelessly for women's rights. They watched the movement grow from that small group that first assembled at Seneca Falls in 1848. As a team, they worked in close harmony toward a common goal, equality for all women. They complimented each other and the two were loyal and loving friends for the rest of their lives.

Sadly, Elizabeth Cady Stanton died on October 26, 1902, eighteen years before women received the vote in the United States.

Angelina Jolie
Actress and Activist

Angelina Jolie, born on June 4, 1975 in Los Angeles, California, is the daughter of actors Jon Voight and Marcia Lynn Bertrand. An accomplished actress herself, she has won an Oscar for her supporting role in *Girl Interrupted* in addition to several Golden Globe Awards.

Early on, Angelina was the consummate rebel. She attended Beverly Hills High School and feeling disaffected, became a cutter. In 1989 at fourteen, she dyed her hair purple and adopted an entirely black wardrobe. She began modeling and appeared on runways in London, Paris and New York. She has never denied her bisexuality admitting to having fallen in love with actress and model, Jenny Shimizu. In a 1997 *Girlfriends* magazine interview, Jolie stated, "I would probably have married Jenny if I hadn't married my husband."

She received her first major role in the B-film *Cyborg 2* in 1993 and her first major film role in 1995's *Hackers*. Good reviews brought more work and it wasn't long before Angelina was a star in her own right. In 1999, Angelina won an Oscar for best supporting actress in *Girl Interrupted*. Today, Jolie is one of the highest paid actors in the film industry.

Early in 2001, Jolie turned her attention to humanitarian work after filming *Laura Croft, Tomb Raider* in Cambodia. In February, she visited refugee centers in Sierra Leone, Tanzania, Cambodia and Pakistan. The influx of Afghani refugees into Pakistan inspired Jolie to donate one million dollars to help alleviate their suffering. By August she had been named a Goodwill Ambassador by the United Nations High Commissioner for Refugees in response to her volunteer work.

Jolie began working to raise political awareness of the plight of refugees around the world. She became an outspoken and effective lobbyist in Washington, D.C.. In 2005, Jolie announced the formation of the *National Center for Refugee and Immigrant Children* and funded it's operation with a $500,000 dollar donation.

Jolie became a member of the Council on Foreign Relations in 2007.

In 2005, while filming *Mr. and Mrs. Smith* with Brad Pitt, she fell in love with her co-star. In spite of making motion pictures, her lobbying efforts and international travel to support her relief efforts, she still found the time to romance the very married Mr. Pitt. Subsequently, Pitt's wife, actress Jennifer Anniston, filed for divorce in March 2005. Their relationship provided fodder for the tabloids and gossip columns for months.

Jolie has one adopted son, Maddox Chivan, a Cambodian orphan she adopted in 2001. She adopted an Ethiopian baby girl and named her Zahara Marley in July 2005. In January 2006, Jolie announced she was pregnant with Pitt's child. On May 27, 2006 Jolie gave birth to their daughter Shiloh in Namibia. Thumbing her nose at the paparazzi, Jolie sold the first pictures of Shiloh to *People* magazine for more than $4 million. International rights brought another $3.5 million. Jolie and Pitt donated all the proceeds to charity. In 2006, Jolie and Pit created the *Jolie/Pitt Foundation* to continue their altruistic global relief efforts. The foundation made contributions of $1 million to both *Doctors Without Borders* and *Global Action for Children*.

In March 2007, Jolie adopted a three year old boy she named Pax Thien from an orphanage in Ho Chi Minh City, Vietnam. On July 12, 2008, Jolie gave birth to twins in Nice, France. This time the baby pictures sold for over $14 million with all the proceeds going directly to the *Jolie/Pitt Foundation*.

Today, Jolie is one of the most widely know celebrities in the world. She was voted the Most Beautiful Woman in the World in a 2006 issue of *People* magazine. In spite of her celebrity, Jolie remains focused on bringing help to refugees and orphans the world over.

Eve
The Mother of Us All

According to the Bible Eve was the mother of us all. That gets her more than honorable mention in this book. Think about it..."Mother of Us All." How could one woman be responsible for all these people. Speaking of people, she was the second person God made after her husband Adam. That gets her more than Honorable Mention, that's for sure. Evidently Adam was lonely in the Garden of Eden and God did some bio- engineering to produce Eve from Adam's rib.

Seems weird to me.

I mean why his rib and why didn't God just make a female without going to all the trouble of sedating Adam and the surgery and all. I mean he's God, seems like there was an easier way to accomplish this. There's a problem with her name, too. It's not clear in the Bible whether her name is Eve or Woman meaning, "from man." Woman seems too generic for a very specific woman.

Besides, Eve sounds a lot friendlier than calling her, "Woman."

The trouble all started with the snake Eve met in the Garden of Eden. This wasn't any ordinary snake...or was it? Some religious texts say the snake wasn't a snake at all, it was really the devil in disguise. Whatever it was Eve met up with in the garden that day, it wasn't good and it talked her into eating an apple from the Tree of Knowledge.

Seems like that should be a good thing, doesn't it?

Where the hell was Adam when all this was going on? Why wasn't he looking out for Eve and why was she so comfortable around that snake? Wasn't she just a little curious about a talking snake? I mean she had to have seen other snakes in the Garden of Eden, did they all talk and if they did, were they as smooth as this particular snake?

I'd like to know because something doesn't seem right here.

Anyhow, Eve knew up front she could eat from any tree but that one. It must have driven her crazy. I can just imagine her obsessing about it. Pacing around the tree mumbling to herself when along comes this fast-talking snake. She doesn't even raise an eyebrow when this snake shows up in the garden.

I don't like snakes.

I am especially cautious around talking snakes. I am naturally wary around any animals that talk. Luckily, I haven't encountered too many of them. Sometimes I wish my dog could talk, but it's probably just as well he doesn't for a lot of reasons. But, like I said, the talking snake doesn't seem to bother her in the least and she engages the snake in conversation.

"Talking snake, huh?" Eve asked.

"Yeah, how's it going?"

"Not bad. What's up?"

"Just hanging out here at the Tree of Life, getting ready to eat an apple."

"We're not supposed to eat the apples from this one."

"Say's who?" inquired the snake.

"God."

"Don't worry about it. He'll never find out."

"Oh, he'll find out somehow. He always does."

The snake looked disgusted and said, "It's not like he's Santa Claus or something." He stuck out his forked tongue at her and smiled as only a snake can. "C'mon," he said brightening, "Try an apple." That's when all the trouble started, all over an apple.

Eve talked Adam into trying the apple, too. At first he was reluctant. "That looks like one of those special apples. You know, from that tree He warned us about. You're not taking apples from that tree are you?"

Eve smiled at Adam. She knew how to get to him.

"Did you notice I'm naked?" she asked.

"You're always naked."

"I know, it's like you don't even care anymore. What does a girl have to do to get your attention these days?"

"You need to go shopping. What do you want? I'm busy."

"Go ahead, try an apple."

"If I do will you leave me alone? I'm trying to take a nap."

"Just one bite," she said and smiled. "For me." When she smiled like that, she knew Adam could deny her nothing.

Besides, she was naked.

That's when all the trouble started. All over an apple.

It wasn't long before she realized that the snake either had no idea what he was talking about or she had been deceived. The first thing that happened was God threw them out of the garden and they had to find work and a place to live. No freebies any more like in the garden.

That wasn't all, God was talking about something called childbirth and original sin. He said Eve was going to enjoy childbirth, but the way he sneered when he told her made her wonder if he was being truthful. Worst of all, Adam and Eve had been equals in the garden, now God was talking about making women subservient to men. At least that's what Adam said God told him.

She gave birth to two sons and it became clear that God had misrepresented the pleasures of childbirth. Some Jewish wags claim Cain wasn't even Adam's son. Some people said his daddy was the snake, or the devil. That more than some innocent apple eating was going on that day in the garden. Depends on what version you read.

That's just what some people said of course. We have no real way of knowing. There was no DNA testing back then to provide conclusive proof. The devil probably wouldn't provide a sample for testing anyhow. I mean you'd think Adam would have a clue, but he doesn't seem capable of figuring out anything by himself.

There were problems between the boys. Cain became a farmer and worked the land. Able was no farmer and he hung out with the sheep, the first shepherd. There came a time when they both needed to make a sacrifice to God who was still angry over the whole apple thing.

Just to stir up some trouble between the two brothers who didn't need much provocation, He showed preference for Able's sacrifice of sheep. Evidently he just shrugged his shoulders when he saw the grain Cain had left for him. Who could know that God wasn't a vegan?

Those Buddhist and Hindu Gods only eat veggies, but not this one.

None of this endeared Able to Cain and it wasn't long before he went looking for him. There was an ugly confrontation and Cain slew Able. Remember, there's a strong possibility that the devil is his daddy. Killing his brother certainly isn't a Christian thing to do, but there weren't any Christians yet at this point in history so he kinda got away with it.

Eve isn't talked about much after this. I mean she's never made Saint Eve or anything like that. There aren't any squares or holidays named after her. She's seems to be pretty much ignored except for the night before Christmas was named for her.

I'm serious. Look it up.

Sharon Osbourne
The Mistress of Oz

Sharon Osbourne is both a real mom and a television mom

There's as big a difference between Ozzy Osbourne and Ozzie Nelson as there is between Sharon Osbourne and Harriet Nelson. First off, Sharon wouldn't be caught dead in one of Harriet's dresses unless she was going to a Halloween party. Harriet wouldn't have dressed like Sharon unless she had taken a new job she couldn't talk about on fifties television.

Then there's the husband issue, too. Ozzie Nelson wasn't bleeped so much it was difficult to follow the conversation. In fact Ozzie was never bleeped. Even when the other Ozzy isn't bleeped, he's unintelligible. It's like he's the poster boy for substance abuse. If it weren't for Sharon, Ozzy couldn't find his #@* with both hands.

Well, you know what I mean.

Sharon would have her hands full just taking care of Ozzy, but she's got three children, too. Real kids fathered by Ozzy, with his genes. Makes you wonder what shape his genes are in after forty years of partying on every substance known to man. I mean, for awhile, he was in communication with Satan when he wasn't biting off bat heads or dove's heads or whatever it was that was unfortunate enough to fall into his grasp.

Remember that Sharon is the smart one in this family.

Sharon Rachel Osbourne was born October 9, 1952 in London, England. Her father, Don Arden, managed Black Sabbath and it was through him that she met her future husband, Ozzy Osbourne at the tender age of eighteen. When Ozzy lost his job as front man for Black Sabbath, Sharon took over his management, revived his career and eventually married the boss. She proved to be an able businesswoman, as tough as any man, perhaps tougher.

In 1996 Sharon created *Ozzfest* to counter the touring *Lollapalooza* summer rock festival. When she had approached the organizers of Lollapalooza to get Ozzy on the bill, she was turned away. Ozzie was irrelevant and burned out she was told, too old for the new audiences. The continued international success of Ozzfest proves otherwise.

In March 2002 MTV debuted a new reality television show, *The Osbournes* which took place primarily in the Beverly Hills home of Ozzy and Sharon Osbourne. The show was an instant hit, eventually becoming the highest rated show ever presented by MTV. America took the foul talking family to heart.

It was fun to guess what Ozzy was saying...or trying to say.

In 2002, in the midst of producing *The Osbournes*, Sharon was diagnosed with colon cancer. She didn't let it slow her down and her fight against the disease became part of the story line. When chemo and radiation treatments took her hair, she wore wigs. Eventually she beat a form of the disease that normally has less than a 40% survival rate. Since her illness, she has very publicly supported multiple research foundations.

The Osbournes ran for four seasons before the family called it quits in March 2005. Tired of the constant presence of the film crew and intrusion into their lives, it was time to move on. In 2003 while the Osbournes was still in production, Sharon premiered her own talk show, The Sharon Osbourne Show. In spite of initial success, the show only lasted one season.

In June 2007, Sharon premiered as a judge on *America's Got Talent* replacing vocalist Brandy. In spite of friction with her co-judges, Sharon has continued appearing on the show at least through the 2010 season.

Somewhere in the midst of all this frantic activity, Sharon found the time to be a mother, something she has in common with many of the women in this book.

Aimee, born September 2, 1983 in London, the oldest of the Osbourne children is the invisible child on *The Osbournes*. For some strange reason she thought her life might be better without the intrusion of cameras or being identified with her siblings or parents. She's the only one of the immediate family who hasn't spent time in rehab. Maybe her extensive vocabulary prevented her from effectively communicating with the rest of her family.   Perhaps she is unable to enunciate her words as well as Ozzy.

It's unlikely don't you think?

The next oldest of the Osbourne children is Kelly.   Born in Westminster, London England on October 27, 1984, she has become a celebrity in her own right. When the family moved from a country estate in England to Beverly Hills, Kelly found herself right in her element. She'd been riding the tour bus since she was an infant. Growing up in the world capital of partying with a rock star for a father, Kelly didn't fail to disappoint as a party animal.

Kelly partied in the clubs of L.A. and London much to the delight of the paparazzi. She partied on the reality show *The Osbournes*.   She did music videos, films, fashion design and recorded her first album, *Shut Up!*

Jack Osborne was born on November 8, 1985 in London. He was diagnosed as having ADD and dyslexia before he was ten.   He was seventeen when *The Osbournes* premiered on MTV and it made him a star. The show led to additional small parts in both movies and television. By the time he was fourteen years old,

Jack, like his sister Kelly, was a partier. On April 21, 2003, Jack was admitted to rehab addicted to OxyContin. Since seeking treatment he has successfully managed to stay sober.

Jack likes his piercings and tattoos. He has a large dragon on his back in addition to many others including one that depicts a heart with "Mum" spelled out across it. In a charming father-son moment, both Ozzy and Jack had matching Smiley Faces tattooed on their kneecaps.

Sharon Osbourne certainly has led a whirlwind life. She admits to having spent more than $500,000 on cosmetic surgery in recent years. She and Ozzy are among the richest citizens in England owning palatial homes both there and in California. She has more energy than many women half her age.

Maybe we should all spend a little time in rehab.

Queen Victoria
Mother of Europe

We often associate the word "Victorian" with prudery and an archaic style of architecture. Victoria, Queen of the United Kingdom of Great Britain and Ireland and Empress of India, ruled longer than any English monarch beating her grandfather George III's record by three days. She became queen upon reaching the age of eighteen and was coronated on June 28, 1838. She ruled an English empire that stretched around the globe and included Canada, India and Australia not to mention large tracts of Africa and the Asian continent. Victoria reigned over England longer than any other English monarch.

Her father, the Duke of Kent, was the fourth son of George III. All his older brothers had produced heirs and all those children had died leaving Victoria next in line for the throne after George IV's short reign. Victoria's father died within a year after she was born leaving her in the care of her mother, the Duchess of Kent. A controlling, power hungry mother, the Duchess forced the young Victoria to share her bed every night until she was eighteen. After an isolated childhood, her only friend a King Charles spaniel, Victoria was filled with resentment when she took the throne.

The duchess tried to get Victoria to accept her lover, Sir John Conroy, as her personal secretary in order to control the young woman, but she refused. When Victoria took power, she made herself unavailable to her mother and Sir John, banishing them from her presence.

Victoria was a beautiful young woman, not the dowdy matron dressed in mourning we tend to remember from later in her life. After being shut away since birth, Victoria was ready for some fun.

She met her future husband, Albert of Saxe-Coburg-Gothburg, a year before her coronation in 1837 but was in no immediate hurry to get married after the cloistered existence her mother had forced upon her. Victoria was as taken by the handsome young Albert as he was by her. In an era when marriages of the upper class, especially royalty, were often arranged for economic and political purposes, theirs was a love match first, a political alliance second. Victoria adored Albert and her diaries are full of entries supporting this. She was struck by the young German's blue eyes and his easy going manner. She was only three months older than Albert and they were well matched in personality and demeanor.

No one seemed to mind that they were first cousins.

Language was no barrier to love. Victoria spoke only German until three years of age when she was taught English and French. Throughout her life, Victoria, queen of the vast British Empire spoke primarily German in private. She was fluent in English, but she had a German accent.

Victoria and Albert were married on February 10, 1840 in St. James Palace, London. They wasted no time starting a family, eventually having nine children.

Their first child, a daughter they named Victoria was born November 21, 1840. She married the Crown Prince of Prussia who later became Fredrick, Emperor of Germany and King of Prussia.

Their son, Victoria's grandson, became Kaiser Wilhelm II, the last monarch of Germany and one of the major combatants of WWI.

Born November 9, 1841, Edward Albert, was known to his family as "Bertie." Bertie was described as affable and possessing what we would today call people skills. In 1860, he undertook a tour of Canada and the United States. He was met by enthusiastic crowds and became known for his charm. He would become King Edward VII in 1901, but due to his mother's long life, he would only reign for nine years before dying in 1910.

Princess Alice was born on April 25, 1843 in London at Buckingham Palace. At the age of twenty-one she nursed her father, Prince Albert, as he lay dying from typhoid fever. She married Prince Louis of Hesse, an impoverished aristocrat, in July 1862 when her mother, Victoria was still in deep mourning for Albert.

Alice was a supporter of Florence Nightingale and worked tirelessly to improve the situation of wounded German soldiers. Tragically, in 1878 at the age of thirty-five, she died of diphtheria.

Born with a friendly nature and affable personality, Prince Alfred was affectionately called "Affy" by the family. He traveled the world representing the British royal family at far flung outposts of the empire. He finished his days as the Duke of Saxe-Coburg and died in 1900, one year before his mother the queen.

Princess Helena, the fifth of Victoria and Albert's children was born at Buckingham Palace on May 25, 1846. Known by the German "Lenchen," Helena was raised with the rest of the royal children. By all accounts, she was not an attractive woman and Victoria had a difficult time finding her a suitable husband. She spent a good part of her life promoting nursing. She died on June 9, 1929 at the age of seventy-seven in London.

The fourth born of Victoria and Albert's daughters, Princess Louise, was artistic and active in the fledgling women's movement much to Victoria's displeasure. When Albert died in 1861, Louise rejected the long period of mourning, which further alienated her from Victoria. She was married in 1871 to John, Marquess of

Lorne. When he died in 1914, Louise moved to Buckingham Palace and was rarely seen in public again. She died at the palace in 1939 at the age of ninety-one.

Prince Arthur was born on May 1, 1850 at Buckingham Palace. From an early age, he seemed destined for a military career. He attended the Royal Military College at Woolwich before entering the army as a lieutenant in Corps of Royal Engineers. What followed was a long and exemplary military career that took Arthur all over the world. From 1911 to 1916, Arthur was governor General of Canada. Even though he had officially retired in 1928, Arthur became active again at the beginning of WWII. He died in January 1942 at the age of ninety-one.

Born in 1853, Prince Leopold, was the youngest son of Albert and Victoria. Diagnosed as a hemophiliac when just a baby, Victoria kept him close by her side, spoiling and doting on the boy. Finally escaping Victoria's grasp by marrying, ill health plagued Leopold. When he went to the south of France to escape London's winter cold in 1884, he slipped and fell injuring his knee. He was given morphine for the pain and a glass of wine to wash down his dinner. The combination of the two resulted in his death at the age of thirty.

Princess Beatrice, whom Victoria called "Baby" was the youngest of her nine children. She was born on April 14, 1857. The queen kept Beatrice close her entire life, discouraging her from marrying. When she finally insisted, Victoria agreed on the condition that she and her new husband, Prince Henry of Battenberg, live close by and she continue in her role as Victoria's closest attendant. After Victoria's death in 1901, Beatrice continued on as the executor of her mother's papers. She died on October 26, 1944.

Victoria was referred to as "The Grandmother of Europe." The marriages of her nine children to other royal houses of Europe guaranteed a large extended family. She had forty-two grandchildren, two of which became European monarchs and were among the principal combatants of WWI, Kaiser Wilhelm and King George

V. Granddaughter Alexandra married Czar Nicolas II, the last Russian Czar.

As a woman, none have wielded more power than Victoria. As a mother, she was an extraordinary woman who led a long, remarkable life. In addition to her children, Victoria's other lifelong obsession was her beloved Albert whom she loved passionately until his death and spent the remainder of her days mourning.

Susan Smith
Mother, Monster, Victim?

You would be hard pressed to find a mother more deserving of the title "Worst Mother" than Susan Smith in recent history. On Tuesday, October 25, 1994, Smith drowned her two young sons in a rural South Carolina lake by launching her car into the water with the two boys strapped into their car seats. When questioned by the police, she said a black man had carjacked her and taken them both with her car. The police found her story suspicious from the beginning and her assertion that it was a black man that had taken her children brought the case to the national media's attention.

It takes a special kind of mother to murder her own children. Unfortunately, it happens all too often. When it happens in multiples as it did in this case, it is especially distressing. When you add the racial overtones as she did when she accused a black man of carjacking her, it becomes particularly ugly.

Susan Vaughn Smith, was born in Union, South Carolina, a mill town, on September 26, 1971, the youngest of Linda Vaughn's three children. Susan has two brothers, Michael and Scotty. Their parents marriage was tempestuous, marred by her father Harry's alcoholism and depression caused by his obsession with his wife's alleged infidelity. Violence was a part of the children's daily lives. When Linda filed for divorce, Harry quit his job, moved out and began to drink heavily.

Just before Christmas 1977, Linda married Bev Russell, a local businessman. Russell was a member of the advisory board of the Christian Coalition and. the South Carolina State Republican executive committeeman. She immediately moved out of the small home she had shared with her husband and into the affluent Russell's home in Mount Vernon Estates. When Harry found out, he became even more depressed. He eventually killed himself on January 15, 1978, a little over a month after the divorce was final.

Susan was six years old.

The quiet little girl became even more introspective after her father's suicide.

Her most treasured possessions were a recording of Harry's voice and coin collection. She was a good student and active in extra-curricular activities. She was friendly and well liked by other students. She enjoyed male attention and was known to occasionally dress provocatively. It wasn't long before she began to seek her stepfather's attention.

When she turned sixteen, she got what she wanted.

It had started with him touching her, but it wasn't long until it progressed to intercourse. She told her mother and high school counselor and a complaint was filed with the Sherriff's Department but nothing much was done. Bev moved out of the house for a while, but it wasn't long before he was back and he pursued a sexual relationship with his step-daughter with even greater enthusiasm.

A year later, Susan reported Bev again with similar results. Her mother wouldn't support the allegations and accused her of trying to undermine the family.

Susan took a job as a cashier at the local Winn-Dixie. She was a hard worker and bright. It wasn't long until she was promoted to head cashier and then book keeper. Soon, she was having an affair with a married co-worker in addition to her continuing relationship with her step-father. At that point, she began sleeping with another co-worker, became pregnant and had an abortion quickly followed by a suicide attempt. After a month's stay in a psychiatric hospital she returned to her job at Winn-Dixie and met her future husband.

She and David Smith had attended Union High School together. When they met at work, Smith was engaged to be married to another woman. When Susan returned to her job at Winn-Dixie from the hospital, Smith broke off his engagement and began to see Susan. It wasn't long before she was pregnant and the couple married on March 15, 1991.

On October 10, 1991, Susan gave birth to their first son, Michael. By the following spring, the marriage was falling apart and David Smith moved out. Susan resumed an affair with one of her co-workers while continuing to have sex with her husband and surprisingly enough, her step-father, Bev Russell.

In November of 1992, Susan found herself pregnant again and attempted another reconciliation with David. On August 5, 1993, Susan gave birth to Alexander Tyler, but within a month, the couple separated again and Susan, not wanting to continue to work with David at Winn-Dixie, resigned her bookkeeping position.

She took a job at a local manufacturer, Conso Products and worked her way up to the executive secretary position. Her new boss, the President and CEO of Conso, J. Carey Findlay was happy with her work and Susan found herself in a new world of affluence. When she met the owner's bachelor son, Tom Findlay, she set her sights on him, convinced she could land Union's most eligible bachelor. By January 1994, she was dating him, but he remained noncommittal much to her disappointment.

That spring, Susan and David gave it another try, but after a few months she announced she was done trying and wanted a divorce. By the next year she was pursuing Tom Findlay again, convinced she could get him to marry her.

Somehow, she knew he wanted it as much as she did, the problem was, she was dead wrong.   By fall, he sought to end their relationship.

He was a gentleman and he wanted to let her down easy.   He wrote her a letter that was supportive, but he firmly stated that their affair was over.   Among the reasons he mentioned were that he didn't want children and he certainly had no intention of raising another man's children.

In the letter, Findlay told her, "If you want to catch a nice guy like me one day, you have to act like a nice girl. And you know, nice girls don't sleep with married men."   He was referring to her indiscretion with a married friend of his.

She began to take time off work to drink and consider her situation.   On the morning of Tuesday October 25, 1995 Susan dropped her two boys off at daycare and went to work at Conso.   At lunch, she joined a group that included Tom Findlay for lunch at a nearby restaurant.   She was uncharacteristically quiet

She didn't return to work from lunch and picked her boys up from daycare.   She returned to Conso and left her children with a friend in the parking lot while she went inside to appeal to Tom Findlay again. Tom immediately hustled her outside the building and she went home.

Later that evening, she woke the two boys and put them in their car seats. Suicidal, she began to drive around with no clear destination. It wasn't long before she found herself at John D. Long Lake outside Union. She drove onto the boat ramp and got out, her children asleep in their car seats. She set the parking brake, put the transmission in drive and got out of the car. When she released the parking brake the car took off down the ramp into the water. It floated for a while and the wind caused it to drift from shore before slowly sinking beneath the surface. She stood and watched from the ramp.

She had to be able to hear her children's screams as they drowned.

From the lake, Susan ran to a nearby home for help. She told the couple that she had been carjacked by a black man who had dumped her from the car and now had her children. Trying to calm the hysterical woman, the couple called the police and a frantic search for the children started.

The initial search was widened and local lakes including the one with her car at the bottom were dragged. It was missed because it had drifted so far from shore before sinking. Over the next nine days the police continued to interrogate Susan and David with the aid of a lie detector. David passed the lie detector test. Susan, however, did not.

Initially basking in the limelight of the media and concerned how she appeared on camera, Susan seemed to be enjoying her fifteen minutes of fame more than a grieving mother should. She played to the camera and enjoyed being the center of attention at press conferences.

On November 3, 1994, Susan broke down and admitted what she had done to Sherriff Howard Wells of the Union County Sherriff's Department. She told him in detail how she had murdered her children. After a highly publicized trial, she was declared guilty of the murder of her two sons and sentenced to thirty years.

There were so many victims.

Television Moms

Television is part of American culture and it has been for over half a century. Through the years there have been many television mothers who became icons of American popular culture. Most television moms were put up on a pedestal but not quite all. Occasionally we would have the anti-mom like *Roseanne* and *Married With Children's*, Peg Bundy representing the dark side of American motherhood, but for the most part, our examples have been healthy, if not humorous.

Timmy and Lassie's mom was not only the epitome of the rural American mother, she able to read a dog's mind on a regular basis. If you're really old like me, you'll remember that Lassie's original boy wasn't Timmy, it was Jeff Miller. Lassie lived with Jeff, Jeff's mother and his grandfather. Jeff had a mom but no father. Timmy's parents adopted him, but I don't recall an episode where Timmy and Lassie set out to find his birth mother. It wasn't done back then or at least no one talked about it.

Lucille Ball and Harriet Nelson actually raised their children on television where they joined them on their shows as recurring characters. The Nelson boys grew up on Ozzie and Harriet. Ricky Nelson the child actor became Rick Nelson the rock and roll star while his mom, Harriet, beamed on the sidelines. Little Ricky was Lucy's frequent companion on *I Love Lucy*.

There are plenty of cartoon moms, too, more than we'll cover here. Wilma Flintstone and Betty Rubble may be two of the most famous. Their children, Pebbles and Bam Bam have marketed everything from vitamins to breakfast cereal. Marge Simpson is busy with her three children, Bart, Lisa and baby Maggie. It's amazing that she has any energy left for her beloved husband, Homie.

There are television mothers like Liv Soprano who plot to kill their own children. Liv dies before succeeding in murdering Tony. When Tony uncovers their plot, he doesn't start planning a big Mother's Day celebration and he makes you wonder if he's planning to whack his own mom in retaliation.

Here they are for your amusement, the Television Moms.

June Cleaver
Beaver's Mom

When *Leave it to Beaver* first aired in 1957, Barbara Billingsly portrayed June Cleaver, mother of two boys, Wally, twelve, the oldest and in eighth grade, and the show's namesake, Beaver, seven and in the second grade. Arguably, June was **the** television mother of the late fifties and early sixties. Married to Ward, the mother of Wally and Theodore (usually called "the Beav" or "Theodore" when he was in trouble, but never, ever, Ted) dispensed motherly love and wisdom to her two boys on *Leave it to Beaver* from October 1957 until June 1963. The much beloved June, occasionally frustrated, but never angry to the point of losing her temper, was the fictional role model for many American mothers of that era, dispensing motherly wisdom by the bucket.

At a time in our history when women were not encouraged to express their opinions, June Cleaver was outspoken. On the subject of child rearing or morality, she could be adamant when discussing the boys' behavior and the consequences of that behavior with Ward. No pushover when it came to raising her boys, June could be a stern disciplinarian. Although she relied on Ward to administer punishment, she could always be counted on to be fair. There was no corporal punishment, she was not a traditionalist. She was exploring the new ideas concerning child rearing put forth by Dr. Benjamin Spock in his 1946 bestseller, *The Common Sense Book of Baby and Child Care*. June was the child of Victorians who shunned their strict regimen of child rearing for the gentler, more contemporary thinking of Dr. Spock. Instead of a trip to the woodshed, she was more inclined to communication and decidedly non-physical means of punishment such as confining the guilty party to their room.

June Cleaver was hot!

Underneath the impossibly long dresses she wore, we boys suspected there lurked the body of a black and white chorus girl. Understand, there were no topless or nude dancers in the fifties and we had to work with what we had. She was slim and tall and wore heels and pearls daily to attend to her mothering and household chores. Our mothers wore dresses too, but it wasn't the same. June had poise and grace. Her hair was perfect. She was always impeccably groomed in an era when women wore dresses to vacuum the house.

It wasn't that our mothers lacked poise and grace it was...well, they were our mothers. June was like a dream mother, almost too pretty to look at without blushing. She was the kind of mom that the other guys would gather at your house just to be around her, to take in the aroma of her perfume and the cookies baking in the oven. She held her nose ever so slightly in the air, not out of snobbery, but from her awareness of posture, a slight smile creased her face.

It wasn't sexual the way we related to her. We were too young for that back then anyhow. Sex was still a taboo subject matter in 1959. Our admiration was sincere and pure. June Cleaver was an impossible ideal that our real-life mothers could never live up to. She was the uber-mother without equal, if she had flaws, they were so inconsequential as to be overlooked. She erred on the side of reason and never over-reacted to the situation.

June's only lack of judgment involved her children's friends. She tolerated Eddie Haskell. She didn't like him, but she tolerated him. I never understood why. I don't think I'd want Eddie Haskell to be hanging around with my kid. Especially since it's obvious that June knows he's a sleaze ball in the making. I didn't like Eddie then, I don't like him now. I wouldn't want him in my house.

It was only a matter of time before Eddie would show up at the local Holiday Inn bar all lounge lizarded up and on the make. June could see this, but chose not to do anything about it. If she wasn't so exemplary in every other aspect of child rearing, her toleration of Eddie would be an unforgivable act of negligent parenting. We'll never really know the long term negative effects of Wally's relationship with Eddie. We can only speculate.

Larry Mondello, Whitey and Lumpy Rutherford round out the regular friends. Larry was kind of a fat, whiny kid that always seemed to be steering the Beav wrong. Beaver didn't get it though, and he continued to hang out with him in spite of repeated incidents that led to him being confined to his room. Whitey was, as his name implies, kinda like white bread, a real Caucasian. He was easy to miss in a crowd, he just disappeared. He was real blonde. Might have been an albino for all we knew with black and white television. We didn't care, no one had anything against albinos anyhow. Back then, my father warned us against the negroes. I was only seven in 1959 and didn't know any negroes so I didn't lose any sleep over it. There were none on television that I recall except Amos and Andy and they were funny in a politically incorrect way. I don't remember him saying anything about albinos...or midgets either.

Anyhow, my mother set me straight on all that stuff.

Lumpy was kinda stupid. Big and stupid, that's how I remember him. What's really crazy is that his father, Fred, sings his praises in public, but browbeats him in private and calls him a loser.

Just makes Ward and June look even better.

As Wally and the Beav got older, June got a little smarter and a little more independent. She occasionally took matters into her own hands, not waiting for Ward's input. Towards the end of the show's run, she would occasionally lose the housedress and appear in tastefully cut slacks like Mary Tyler Moore was doing on *The Dick Van Dyke Show*.

If *Leave it to Beaver* had run another ten years, June would have been wearing designer jeans with four inch heels and Ward would've been history. She'd be vegetarian, running a small art gallery in Soho and living with her musician lover.

...or perhaps not!

Roseanne Conner
Dysfunction Anyone?

Roseanne Barr's Roseanne Conner character was the anti-Christ to Barbara Billingsly's June Cleaver. These two may be the most famous television mothers ever. Barr's roughness would have horrified Billingsly's Cleaver. They couldn't be more different or have played more important roles in the development of the portrayal of families on television. As demure as Billingsly's portrayal of June Cleaver was, Barr's Roseanne character was equally loud and crude. It would be hard to imagine her saying, "Well, Beaver, would you like to talk about it?" Roseanne Conner was much more direct. She would demand your full attention.

Roseanne wasn't a stay at home Mom. In the first season, she worked in a plastics factory with her sister Jackie and friend, the somewhat dim-witted Crystal. George Clooney played her boss, Booker. The season ends with them leading a walk out, which leads to the closure of the plant and the loss of everyone's jobs.

Rebel without a job!

Whew! Can't see June Cleaver doing something like that. Hard to imagine her even working, let alone being a militant labor leader like some kind of outrageous, menopausal Norma Rae. When Roseanne says, "We're walking!" It's believable. June couldn't pull it off. When *Roseanne* premiered in 1988, there had been nothing like it on television before. She was a loud mouthed, opinionated woman who didn't take grief from anyone.

Her husband, Dan Conner, a gentle giant, tried to be the voice of reason. You didn't question the match. It seemed natural. Neither of them were Rhodes Scholars, but deep down inside, they exemplified the struggle of middle America to survive if not prosper. In spite of financial setbacks, the Conner family never loses hope or sinks into despair. Dan was self-employed as a contractor, struggling between jobs. Roseanne didn't work for extras or because she wanted to, she worked because she had to. They needed that steady income that Dan, despite his heart of gold and best intentions, couldn't provide. Ward Cleaver came home from work to dinner every night dressed in a suit. His hands, soft and clean. The Cleavers didn't eat dinner in the kitchen, they took their supper in the dining room.

Roseanne thought they were lucky to be eating dinner at all. She didn't care much how Dan was dressed. She was just happy he was dressed. In spite of all his failings, Dan Conner was Roseanne's man and she made sure he knew it. She never questioned his sincerity or devotion. They were in it together, for better or worse, until the end.

Unless something really weird happened.

The Conners were close to the bottom of the food chain and they knew it. They struggled, knowing that for them, it was almost impossible to escape their dismal, desperate existence. Roseanne still had hope that her family could escape their lives of dreadful mediocrity. She had hope for her children even as she saw all the frightening signs of what would be their reality before they were old enough to leave the house.

Roseanne didn't pull any punches, she was tough, she had to be. She knew her children would have to be hard to survive and what she saw scared her. Becky, her oldest, was oblivious. Her world revolved around her boyfriend, Mark, her survival skills almost non-existent. Darlene her middle child is dark and wry. As her character develops from smart mouthed child to dark, sarcastic, nihilist, her depth is revealed. The only one of the children smart enough to actually have a chance to succeed, in one episode she is referred to as, "Death" by a commercial director.

The youngest child, a son called DJ, might be hopeless, but no one is willing to admit it to themselves. Silently, though they don't give up on DJ, both Roseanne and Dan have accepted that their son's future is not bright.

There were no subjects out of bounds. There were episodes covering Darlene's first period, Becky's request for birth control and DJ's fascination with masturbation. Martin Mull appeared as Roseanne's gay boss, Leon. Roseanne took on a lesbian partner, Nancy, played by Sandra Bernhard, at the restaurant. Roseanne used them as foils, but the humor wasn't viscous or offensive and both Mull and Bernhard got in plenty of licks of their own.

It is doubtful June Cleaver was acquainted with any lesbians and I don't recall any episodes where she, or Beaver for that matter, had any serious dealings with lesbians. With the exception of June, women were relegated to relatively minor roles on *Leave it to Beaver*. When you did see other women, they always seemed to be wearing white gloves, hats and going to tea. It was unlikely they were lesbians. Real lesbians ride motorcycles and wear construction boots and flannel shirts. June probably didn't even own a flannel shirt. I'd be surprised if she rode a motorcycle.

Roseanne drank beer with Dan, Jackie and Crystal. I think they might have smoked pot on one episode. She definitely wasn't girly and I suspect she had a lot more fun than June Cleaver. Roseanne probably didn't own any white gloves...or a hat. Roseanne always looked out of sorts in her waitress uniform. It's hard to picture her getting ready for work pulling on a pair of pantyhose. She isn't masculine by any means, but she isn't overly feminine either. More important is that she is comfortable in her own skin, no matter its condition.

The Conner family pursued the American dream of owning their own business when they bought the diner where Roseanne had been working as a waitress. They renamed it, The Lanford Lunch Box and it gave her someplace to go after she lost her other job at the plastics plant. Like most new, small businesses, their restaurant eventually went bust, but they had made enough money off the television show that no one really cared. Her husband, Dan, left her and changed his name to John Goodman. He makes movies now.

Some of his movies have been really funny.

Roseanne the television show went into syndication and Roseanne Barr accomplished what her character never could. She escaped mediocrity and almost certain economic struggle. Barr went on to a career in movies and comedy, but you don't see much of her any more.

She doesn't need the money.

Wilma Flintstone
Fred's Alice Kramden

What kind of name is Wilma in this day and age? I mean really, who names their beautiful baby daughter, Wilma? It was an odd name even back in the stone age when the Flintstones was set. Her best friend was named Betty. That's not so bad. Betty sounds perky and friendly. Wilma sounds dour and frumpy.

Luckily, Wilma was anything but dour and frumpy.

Wilma had a nice shape, was generally happy and well-adjusted considering she had to put up with Fred. She was a lot smarter than Fred, too. It upset Fred sometimes, but in the end, he knew it was true. Some people might think they were an odd match, but Wilma admired Fred's strength the moment she met him. He made her feel secure when he was around. In spite of their constant bickering, Wilma and Fred loved each other. They were the first television couple who slept in the same bed.

Some people said she dyed her hair red, that she was really a dishwater blonde. Her detractors said she did it to attract men, that she liked to be the center of attention. I don't believe it's true. Those are just catty and jealous remarks made by the same people who despise her for her Barbie-like figure.

The one scary thing about Wilma is her eyes. I'd like to say she was a green-eyed, red head, but I can't. She doesn't really have any eyes. Neither does Barney. Everyone else has eyes, even Dino, their pet somethingasaurus has eyes but not Wilma and Barney. They just have these black holes where their eyes should be.

What is the significance of this anomaly?

Was she, like Barney, undeserving of eyes? Are these stone aged black holes that allow us to see into the depths of their souls? Both Pebbles and Bam Bam have eyes. Why is it that Wilma and Barney's offspring have eyes, but they don't? Is there some dark secret? Maybe they're aliens or something. When you look at her up close, it's kinda creepy.

Wilma avoided crowds and Betty is her only real friend. Wilma and Betty are as close as sisters. They rarely argued about anything and are truly each other's best friend. For the most part, Fred and Barney provided the only conflict in their lives and the women usually prevailed in those situations by conspiring against them.

Wilma worked in the home and was a good wife and mother with nineteen sixties sensibilities during the Stone Age. Most nights when Fred came home from a hard day at the quarry, she had dinner on the table, maybe a big slab of Brontosaurus ribs to make him happy. Wilma wasn't a gourmet cook, but she knew what Fred liked. She tried to get him to eat more green vegetables, but he always left them on his plate. In spite of her best efforts, he remained a meat and potatoes kind of guy.

She has a vitamin named after her, sort of. As one of the Flintstones characters, she is replicated as a Flintstone vitamin. There aren't many mothers out there that can say that they're depicted on a drug or have one named for them. I mean like, none that I can think of off-hand. Is Valium a woman's name?

One disturbing aspect of Wilma's character is that not only did she smoke cigarettes, but she endorsed and advertised them as well. She and the rest of the cast smoked and promoted Winstons on the show from 1960 until 1962. It was common to see the characters kicking back and enjoying a smoke in the comfort of their living rooms. Winston withdrew their advertising in 1963 when Wilma became pregnant with Pebbles. Wilma quit smoking during her pregnancy, but Fred continued off camera. He was afraid he'd lose his husky voice if he were to quit. In spite of Wilma's best efforts and his doctor's strong objections, Fred continues to smoke two packs a day to this very day.

No one really knows how old Wilma is. It's like that with a lot of women, especially in show business. It's some kind of closely guarded secret or something with some women and Wilma is one of them. If she were in her early child bearing years in 1963, she'd probably be in her late sixties or early seventies now. I can picture her turning off her hearing aid when Fred comes home from the Loyal Order of Water Buffaloes, stinking of beer and cigarettes and wearing that stupid hat. She doesn't object to the lodge because it gets him out of the house for a few hours and gives her some private time.

Wilma's whole life changed when Pebbles was born. The beautiful baby girl melted Fred's heart immediately and he became the doting father to Wilma's practical, loving mother. In spite of having all the latest modern conveniences, like a pelican washing machine, being a mother was still hard work. Wilma threw herself into mothering and coincidently, her best friend Betty adopts baby Bam Bam about the same time, further cementing the women's bond.

There was one problem though.

Pebbles never seemed to grow up. I mean she's been baby Pebbles as long as I can remember. She should be near fifty by now. How does she do that? There have been actresses who portrayed Pebbles in movies after the original show went off the air in 1966, but I know they're not the real Pebbles. They're just actresses pretending to be the real Pebbles. Kinda like a mall Santa.

Isn't Wilma really tired by now?

I mean taking care of an infant for a couple of years with the expectation that eventually, the child will grow up is one thing, but to be perpetually changing diapers is another. Sure Pebbles is cute, but after thirty, forty years of catering to her every whim, it would get old for even the most patient of mothers. From all appearances, Pebbles is taking after Fred in the brains department and Wilma finds that particularly disturbing..

The same goes for Bam Bam. Who'd want him around the house all the time with that damn club? Sure, Betty is Wilma's friend, but the kid has strained the relationship. She's always over at the Flintstones with him. All he can say is, "Bam! Bam!" and beat the floor with his club to get attention. Betty is so used to it that she doesn't even notice, but it drives Wilma up the wall. She wants to talk to Betty about it, but is afraid it will start a fight. Anonymously, Wilma sends Betty information on Ritalin and as a friend, urges her to seek help.

Some guys liked Wilma. Other guys liked warm, down to earth, slightly oblivious Betty. It was kinda like the Veronica and Betty thing from *Archie* comic books but different. I liked Wilma. She was always simmering just under the surface and that appealed to me.

Claire Huxtable
Role Model

Phylicia Rashad as Clair Huxtable on *The Cosby Show* is a strong woman who happens to be black. I suspect she'd be a strong woman if she were green or pink.

She and her husband Cliff, portrayed by Bill Cosby, live an upper middle class life in Brooklyn, New York with their five children Sondra, Denise, Theo, Vanessa and Rudy.

Rashad played the role of Clair for eight seasons between 1984 and 1992. Originally, Cosby wanted the character of Claire to be a stay-at-home mom in a struggling blue collar family. He would portray a limo driver. The show's producers, Marcy Carsey and Tom Werner convinced Cosby the show would have more appeal if the family were middle class and the parents professionals. As a result, Cosby's Cliff became an doctor, his wife Clair, an attorney.

Clair is an alpha female, a character trait that both endears her to Cliff and occasionally frustrates him. She runs the house and raises the children in addition to holding down a demanding full time job as an attorney. Her main occupation seems to be as the glue that holds the family together for Claire is a superwoman with priorities.

She puts nothing ahead of her family.

Her oldest daughter, Sondra (Sabrina LeBeauf) has graduated from Princeton and left home. A typical eldest child, she is an over-achiever, focused and brighter than her siblings. Sondra marries in the fourth season, becomes pregnant and names her first two children after South African activists Winnie and Nelson Mandela. She is held up as an example to the other children who sometimes resent her.

Claire's second oldest daughter, Denise (Lisa Bonet), starts the show off as a sixteen year old high school student with the typical problems of a teen. Pretty and popular, she has a new boyfriend pursuing her almost every week. As she grows up on the show, she becomes more serious...and flighty. Claire does what she can to keep her daughter's feet on the ground, but doesn't always succeed. In the third season, Denise leaves home to go to Cliff and Claire's alma mater, Hillman College. She also gets her own show for two seasons called, *A Different World* before returning to the Cosby fold.

Theodore, known as Theo (Malcolm-Jamal Warner), is an athletic girl crazy teen who initially struggles with school. As Claire's only son, his problems are different from her daughter's and he is often referred to his father for advice. Late in the series, when Theo enters college, it is discovered that he is dyslexic. In the end, Theo graduates from college with the intention of helping dyslexic children as a career.

Claire's third daughter, Vanessa (Tempest Bledsoe) is the smart kid, sometimes too smart for her own good. Inquisitive, she pokes her nose into everyone's business and frequently butts heads with her brother Theo. When she isn't fighting with Theo, there is always her youngest sister, Rudy, with which to lock horns.

The baby of the family, Rudith (Keshia Knight Pulliam) nicknamed Rudy, has all the perks associated with her position. She is cute when required to be so on the show. In the beginning, at five years old, her role was almost incidental to the story line, but by the time the show reached its eighth and final season, Rudy was thirteen years old.

One could almost think of Claire Huxtable as being the prototype for Michelle Obama, both are tall, intelligent black women of accomplishment. Claire isn't George Jefferson's "Weezie." This is a woman being held up as a role model, not just for black women, but all women.

There are few serious sit-com moms. Harriet Nelson and June Cleaver were serious, but in a different way. They were likable and you liked them, but you suspected they didn't have much depth. When you meet Claire for the first time, her presence demands respect. You don't know why, but you immediately know she's the level headed one of the bunch. It's not that she's so much smarter than he is, it's that most of what she says is irrefutable, even by Cliff.

When she lectures him on his diet and fondness for junk food, it comes from the heart. It's not nagging, it's based on genuine concern for his health, more than he apparently displays for himself. Being mothered by one's wife is a common sit-com theme as old as the medium itself. Television men seem to require it the way they are so often caricatured.

On television men depend on strong women to help them make it through the day. The women are usually right in the end. Even women like Archie's beloved Edith nurtured their husbands. Though Edith and Claire are at opposite extremes of the spectrum, they have more in common than first meets the eye.

They are both adored by their husbands in a way that is hard for a wife to understand. If the relationship is right, women play a stabilizing role in their husband's lives. When the testosterone begins to rage, when desire overcomes reason, these women are able to calm their beast, to have influence few are capable of exerting over her mate. It doesn't matter if Edith is trying to get Archie to admit that the "coloreds" aren't any different than the two of them or Claire is trying to get Cliff to think about his diet.

The motivation is the same.

The women love and care about their families and they want their husbands to be the best men they can be. Both Claire and Edith know the healing and calming power of a hug. Physical contact is a mighty force.

Claire can tell her husband when he's wrong without fear of retribution. That, unfortunately is not the universal right it should be. Again, there is much in common between the two women and their families. Archie will make more noise than Cliff when Edith chides him, but in the end both men know their wives are right.

And that...is all she really wanted to hear anyway.

Jill Taylor
Married to the Tool Man

Jill Taylor, as portrayed by Patricia Richardson on *Home Improvement* is an "everymom." She's raising three sons and her husband, Tim (Tim Allen). It's difficult to tell who needs more attention. She's diplomatic when she needs to be and firm when required. She experiences a lot of frustration, most of it generated by Tim. She's no stranger to anger either, when Tim makes fun of her on his television show, *Tool Time*, she doesn't take it well and lets him know his comments aren't appreciated in no uncertain terms.

You have to respect a woman who repeatedly stands up for herself to a thoughtless spouse. Tim isn't malicious, he loves Jill, he's just oblivious to the feelings of others. He understands crankshafts and transmissions, his main field of ignorance is in human relations and his relationship with his wife is no different than any of his other relationships. He is adept at making thoughtless remarks and often makes the situation worse trying to extricate himself from the situation. All of this requires a great deal of patience on Jill's part not to mention an unusually large capacity for forgiveness.

When the show first came on the air, Jill was a stay at home television mom. It was a full time job looking after her husband and three young sons. She was an average cook at best and there were numerous jokes made at her expense regarding her cooking expertise or lack thereof.

Jill is the smartest one in the family and certainly brighter than Tim. That's usually the case on television. The wife is the one with the brains more often than not. Occasionally, a couple like Archie and Edith Bunker comes along where they're both hopeless, but not too often. Some like Cliff and Claire Huxtable are equally bright. Most couples fall someplace in between. Tim is not the sharpest tool in the shed if you forgive my pun.

He slaughters the English language and seems to know just enough about everything to get himself in trouble. It doesn't matter whether he's souping up the lawn tractor or altering the garbage disposal to provide "more power," you can bet Tim will somehow turn it into a disaster and if at all possible, Jill will try to save the day if only by being the voice of reason. As the show progressed and the children grew, Jill went back to school and earned a degree in psychology.

She needed it with that bunch.

Her oldest son, Brad (Zachery Ty Bryan), is a jock and almost as smart as his father. Jill is patient with him but recognizes that she's helped create another Tim clone. Tim relates to Brad best, of the three children, they're on the same wavelength. Brad's young, but Tim is just the guy who can help his natural dullness grow and develop into something meaningful...or not.

The middle son, Randy (Jonathan Taylor Thomas) is the smart one of the three children. He got Jill's genes. He's sarcastic just like his dad, but Randy's a lot smarter than his father, Tim or brother Brad and he enjoys toying with both of them. Sometimes he encourages them both to do things he knows will end in disaster just to amuse himself.

The youngest of their three children, Mark (Taran Noah Smith) is the target of abuse from his two older brothers. This is probably the first time that ever happened. Mark was young when the show started and his character was pretty flat during the early seasons. Mark becomes a proto-Goth in later seasons but it wasn't much more than window dressing. He never displayed the emotional range of a hamster in his performances. It's always the quiet ones you have to watch but you watched and watched and he did nothing.

Luckily, he looked good in black.

Jill is no Barbie Doll, she's a real woman, attractive in her own right and on her own terms. She has strengths and weaknesses like everyone. She loves Tim but sometimes wonders if she made the right choice in a mate. Occasionally, she's attracted to a man that makes her question her relationship with her husband. Tim is not above jealousy if Jill pays attention of another man or is the subject of attention herself. Inevitably, in spite of the temptations that come her way, she remains faithful to Tim.

On the other side of the fence is Jill's confidant, Wilson, who dispenses sage advice to anyone who'll listen. Wilson is the smart guy on the show who often sympathizes with Jill's plight and tries to help, usually unsuccessfully. It isn't that his advice to Tim is bad, it's just generally misunderstood. Tim manages to distort Wilson's wisdom almost every time. At least Jill has someone close at hand who understands her predicament and offers her a helping hand and some sympathy when she needs it most.

Sometimes I think Jill sticks around because she finds Tim's antics amusing. He does make her smile on a regular basis, whether it's his faltering command of the English language or his latest project out in the garage, it's never boring being married to Tim. When the couple takes a compatibility test, they find they're not well suited for each other but it doesn't seem to bother Tim at all.

Jill likes opera and doesn't realize that her efforts to get Tim to share her enthusiasm, are in vain. Tim doesn't understand culture nor does he want to. The Detroit Lions and his garage are among the greatest of his interests and there is little room for more. The few times Tim is exposed to culture, it's usually the result of losing a bet to Jill.

Jill has had her temptations. There is a lot of jealousy between the two and she can be as bad as Tim when it comes to being unreasonably possessive. At one point, Tim goes to school with Jill just to keep an eye on her. In one of the later seasons, they go into couples therapy to try and avoid the fate of their recently divorced friends.

In the end, Tim and the entire cast of *Tooltime* walk out on Binford, the show's sponsor. Jill saves the day when she accepts a position in Indiana offered by her former psychology professor. They pack up the house and move everything to Indiana. Eventually, we knew Jill would be the glue that held the family together.

It couldn't end any other way.

Liv Soprano
Bada Bing

Livia Soprano was a unique television mom. The only mother that comes to mind that actually spends time plotting to whack her own son for putting her in the Green Grove nursing home. It's a good thing this was an isolated incident and didn't spawn any copy cat hits or a lot of us might die before our time. Now granted, this was a mob family and I suppose they do these sort of things, but as a rule, we as humans, do not kill and eat our young.

Liv, as she was known, was different. She thrived on misery and complaining. If she had been anyone else, Tony would have made her disappear long ago. He just wouldn't put up with it. His means of dealing with minor irritants was most effective. He put up with her neurotic behavior because she was his mother.

That doesn't mean he liked it though.

This woman is hard to love. Even her own children can't really do it. Her condition is pitiful really, but of her own making.   There is nothing redeeming in her personality.   She never has anything positive to say about anyone or anything. She is manipulative, vindictive and hateful, and those are her good qualities.   If she's friendly, she wants something.   Otherwise she wouldn't bother.

When Tony becomes a silent partner of restaurateur and childhood pal Artie Bucco, he secretly burns the place to the ground for the insurance money.   Artie, believes it was an electrical fire until he visits Liv at the nursing home to deliver some Italian delicacies, and she fills him in on why the restaurant really burned. Understandably,   this   creates   friction between the powerless Artie and his alleged friend, Tony, but it does not produce the revenge she was hoping to inspire.

Not long after, as punishment, Tony sentences his son A.J. to no television or Nintendo and visiting his grandmother at the nursing home every day for two weeks.   It is during one of these forced visits that A.J. tells Livia that he's seeing a counselor.   When she expresses shock at his   revelation,   A.J.   counters   that   his father, Tony, has been seeing a psychiatrist.

Recognizing opportunity when she sees it, Livia turns to Tony's Uncle Junior next. Technically, Junior is running the family, but everyone knows that Tony is the real capo.

During a visit at the nursing home, she expresses concern that her son is visiting a psychiatrist to Junior. This comes as a surprise to Junior, and he is concerned that Tony may be talking about family business with Dr. Melfi. Junior is upset, but not angry enough to kill his nephew, which is what Livia suggests as a traditional and reasonable security precaution.

Livia and Junior are the last of a generation that came of age in the fifties during the glory years of the mob. Tony's father, "Johnny Boy" Soprano, the patriarch of the family, ran his crew with his brother, Junior. When he passed away, Junior took over the family and he and Tony provided for Livia's needs. In spite of the entire extended family's almost constant attention, she is miserable to the point of trying to punish her son by setting him up to be murdered by her brother-in-law.

Ironically, it is the FBI that alerts Tony to his mother's efforts to have him killed. They've had a bug in her assisted living quarters since she moved in and it's proven to be most interesting and informative. Seeing the situation as an opportunity to introduce tension, Tony's FBI handlers play him the tapes from his mother's room to alert and throw him off balance.

As expected, Tony only puts up with this for so long. In spite of talking to Dr. Melfi about his mother to try and reach a peaceful solution to his problem, Tony snaps. This woman absolutely brings out the worst in people. When she has a stroke, Tony presses a pillow to her face. Restrained by emergency room attendants, he disowns her emotionally and financially.

Her relationship with her other children is no better. Liv's youngest daughter and constant source of irritation to Tony, is Janis. Livia enjoys stirring up trouble between Tony and Janis whenever she can. Neurotic Janis always has some unwanted advice for Tony. She has a love/hate relationship with Liv, which she never resolves. When Liv finally dies, it's hard to tell if Janis is grieving her mother or all the unresolved issues between them. We find there's a little of Liv in Janis when she shoots and kills her husband.

Daughter Barbara is happily married and has distanced herself from the family. If she has a relationship with Livia, it is minimal at best. Married outside of the mob, she only attends family functions that are absolutely essential, baptisms, weddings and funerals. Unlike the others, she doesn't stop by Tony's place for Sunday dinner or call to chat. When Tony is shot and almost killed by a delusional Uncle Junior, Barbara helps maintain the vigil at the hospital.

Barbara is a fine example of a child breaking with family tradition. In spite of having a mobster father and a psycho mother, she has adjusted to life and tried to move on, discarding the baggage she was born with as gracefully as possible. The chances are good that her children don't know their cousins very well. Barbara may look at her nephew A.J. with less than affection. She may have perceived him as a young mobster in training.

In the end, we didn't even get a satisfying end to the character of Livia Soprano. The actress who portrayed her, Nancy Marchand, died in the middle of the season's filming. A contrived ending was fabricated and Tony was only left with ugly memories, Janis with unresolved issues and Barbara one step closer to freedom.

I hope her character found peace in the next world because she didn't find it here.

Murphy Brown
Slugger

Murphy Brown, portrayed by Candice Bergen, created a furor when she became an unwed mother on her namesake show in the 1991/92 season. It pushed the show to #3 in the Neilson ratings, and it's momentum continued into the following season where it was #4 for the year. Murphy handled her pregnancy and consequent birth of her son with her usual sardonic wit. It was almost a relief when she finally gave birth and turned her attention elsewhere.

The season's theme even drew a negative response from then Vice-President Dan Quayle, as an attack on family values during a 1992 speech at the Commonwealth Club in San Francisco. Quayle expressed concern that Murphy's single parenthood sent the wrong kind of message to the country. He blamed the recent Los Angeles riots on America's "poverty of values" and suggested that Murphy Brown contributed to the problem by her portrayal of an unwed, professional mother.

He was quoted as saying, "It doesn't help matters," when "a character who supposedly epitomizes today's intelligent, highly paid professional woman" is "mocking the importance of fathers, by bearing a child alone," and dismissing it as a "lifestyle" choice.

Film of Quayle's speech was edited to make it appear as if he believed Murphy Brown were a real person and used on the show. A month later Quayle mistakenly corrected an elementary school student's spelling of the word "potato" as "potatoe" and the show seized the opportunity to have more fun at his expense. References to the Vice-President continued throughout the season much to the consternation of Quayle. Candice Bergen who portrayed Brown, didn't care what the Vice-President thought and *Murphy Brown* turned Quayle's comments into a running joke.

At season's end, Murphy's fictional television news show, FYI, devoted an entire show to the social issue of single motherhood and the dynamic American society that embraces diverse lifestyles, just to tweak Quayle's nose further. Hillary Clinton added to the debate by referring to Quayle and the Bush administration as being, "out of touch with America" in response to Quayle's criticisms. Eventually, Quayle developed a sense of humor about the incident. When asked what his favorite television show was during a Los Angeles interview Quayle quipped, "Murphy Brown...Not!"

The series begins with Murphy's first day back on the job as a reporter for *FYI* after being released from *The Betty Ford Clinic.* Cranky and disagreeable, she is none the less happy to be back. Her old insecurities are still there, but now she must face them alone, without alcohol. Murphy's successful battle with the bottle and the stories of her days as a hard drinker as told by her old friend, Phil the bartender, enliven more than one episode.

Murphy was famous for her turnover of secretaries. During the course of the series, the role of Murphy's secretary was played by ninety-three different actors. Over the years, they were portrayed by Sally Field, Bette Midler, Paul Ruebens (Pee Wee Herman) and John F. Kennedy

Jr. among others. When her son, Avery, was born she began to experience the same problem with nannies that she had with secretaries. Everyone has the occasional problem with daycare, but Murphy's problems were continuous. Eventually she settles on Eldin, her house painter, confident, advisor and handyman, to act as baby Avery's nanny.

By all indications, he is a good choice.

If we judge Murphy by her selection of nannies and handymen, we face some choices. Clearly, of the two, the choice of nanny is by far the most important. The raising of children cannot be taken lightly. Walls can be repainted, a child is more permanent, more fragile and threatened by incompetence. The qualities of a good nanny are not necessarily those of a good house painter or handyman.

Except perhaps in this case.

Turns out that much to everyone's surprise, Eldin knows more about babies than Murphy, substantially more. He spends the next seven seasons as Avery's primary care provider and surrogate father. Not surprisingly, Eldin does such a remarkable job that it makes you wonder if he might have a future with Murphy. Before long, it becomes clear that Murphy is too independent and strong willed to really be any man's wife. She is uncomfortable with the whole concept, barely accepting motherhood as more than an imposition on her busy lifestyle. This doesn't mean she doesn't love Avery, for she does. Murphy is bright enough to know where her talents lie and maternal nurturing isn't part of her skill set. She gives that job to someone more qualified, Eldin. Murphy and Eldin settle into their roles as mother and bearded nanny. Avery is accepting, knowing he is loved by both.

In 1998, the last year of *Murphy Brown's* run, Murphy confronted a new challenge, breast cancer. Her disease dominated the entire last season and was instrumental in raising women's awareness of the dangers of breast cancer. There was a 30% increase in the number of women asking for and receiving mammograms during this period, most of which was attributed to the impact of the story line.

During the course of her treatment for breast cancer, Murphy's friend, news anchor Jim Dial scores Murphy some pot in the park and she uses it to successfully treat the nausea and loss of appetite created by chemo. Showing marijuana in a positive light on the show created another furor. She baited the Bush administration in the episode with a remark about not wanting to try pot because she was afraid Attorney General "Janet Reno would kick my door down." The conservative backlash accused Bergen and Brown of promoting drugs on the show. If her intention was to create debate, she achieved her goal. A mass audience learned that there were uses for marijuana other than getting stoned.

Murphy's parenting skills and social causes notwithstanding, she was indeed unique as a television mom. She was independent and outspoken. She represented the modern career woman of the nineties who tried to have it all. Sometimes Murphy succeeded and sometimes Murphy failed, but she always tried. Murphy didn't listen to people when they said she couldn't do something. She was capable of anything except sustaining a committed relationship with a member of the opposite sex.

And, in the end, that didn't seem to bother her all that much.

Peg Bundy
Shoe Salesman's Wife

Peg Bundy is the kind of woman you meet in a neighborhood bar and before you know it, you've had too much to drink and she has her hand on your thigh. From a man's perspective, you know that if you take her home, you'll regret it. If you don't, you'll always wonder what you might have missed. The big difference between that woman and Peg, is that Peg would never cheat on Al any more than he would cheat on her.

Peg is perpetually horny, but her husband Al doesn't seem to be in a big hurry to do anything about it, which is strange considering how much time he spends looking at magazines with names like *Big Hooters* and going to strip clubs. Al seems interested in sex, just not with Peggy and it is the never ending source of conflict between the two of them.

Peg has hooters of her own, but Al isn't interested in them anymore. In spite of her constant attempts to lure him to the bedroom and seduce him, he steadfastly resists her efforts. Her red hair teased high, Peg wears stretch pants and heels with a push up bra and a top displaying plenty of cleavage, all to no avail. Much to her frustration, Al usually won't touch her. When he does, she chides him for his speed in finishing, but Al doesn't care. He thinks she's lucky he did anything at all. He just shrugs his shoulders and goes back to watching television.

Al's fond of touching himself. He likes nothing better than to kick back on the couch and watch television with his hand down his pants. It always puts a smile on his face, but we're never sure what he's doing down there and it's probably just as well we leave that path unexplored.

It can't be anything good.

If Peg notices, she doesn't say anything. Better to just whine and complain about him and his lousy job at the shoe store. He has never supported her in the manner in which she would like to become accustomed and he doesn't care. Al ignores her whining, which just provokes more of the same. Peg doesn't understand the futility of complaining to someone who just doesn't care. Al just wants to get through the day, go home and have some juice, or if he's lucky a cold beer. Peg wants to go shopping and buy things with Al's hard earned money that they can't afford and don't need.

Peggy is the mother of Kelly and Bud who is the smartest of the Bundys, not like it was a hard race to win or anything. Bud is smarter and more adept at manipulating his parents than his sister Kelly, but it's easy to stand out in this family. In any family other than the Bundy bunch, it's a good bet he'd be locked up for evaluation in an institution somewhere.

Bud is smarter, but he has inherited personality traits from his father that Peg finds disconcerting. Bud is always horny and Peg, seems to find his never ending frustration amusing. He's the kind of kid the other kids beat up because they find him annoying. He's not athletic or smart. Bud's not good looking or talented. Bud is so much like Al in so many ways it's scary. The big difference between father and son is that for a fleeting moment in one Polk High School football game, Al was a hero when he scored the winning touchdown.

Peg's only son will never even have that small opportunity to achieve fleeting fame. His destiny is a life of never ending, brain numbing, mediocrity.

Kelly is a tramp...a dumb one, a really dumb one. Peggy had at least learned to use her sexuality to trap Al in marriage, freeing her from a life of responsibility. Al's youthful randiness had produced two children that Peg considered her meal ticket. If Peggy has taught her daughter anything, it's the power sex has over men. Kelly hasn't made the connection between sex and being responsible for a child's life.

Kelly has learned how to attract men and her provocative dress is a more contemporary version of her mother Peg's attire. Kelly is the neighborhood tramp, but her parents don't seem to care. Al reluctantly accepts her for who she is, but Peg sees herself as a young woman in Kelly.

Peg's maiden name is Wanker. It's a bad joke based on British slang for a masturbator. She's proud to be a Wanker and seemingly unaware of her name's heritage. The name is brought up on a semi-regular basis for cheap laughs, but there's nothing cheap about Peggy. Just ask Al. He's been supporting her and her bad habits for years.

"Oh, Al."

Depending on the inflection this phrase could have many meanings. Sometimes it was affectionate, others it could be demanding or complaining. Behind all the posturing and stereotypes, Al and Peggy love each other. It doesn't matter if their daughter is a tramp or Al works in a shoe store. To Peggy, Al will always be the football hero who swept her off her feet.

Peggy Wanker could have married a lot of boys, but she chose Al Bundy. There was no college in their future. In fact, there was no real future in their future. They were both condemned to lead nearly meaningless lives together and raise children that quite likely will follow in their footsteps. Still, they cling to each other. They are each other's only reality.

Peggy and Al make us laugh because we see how easy it might be to slip into a version of that reality. Maybe a lot of us see a little of ourselves in them. Not a lot, just a little. It would be hard to replicate the pair. It's almost a warning against dissatisfaction in our own lives.

Hopefully when we look at our children, we don't see a Bud or Kelly. When we look at our spouses, we don't see a Peggy or Al and the acceptance of hopelessness. If nothing else, the Bundys should make us realize that things could always be worse.

Marge Simpson
Yellow Skin, Blue Hair

You don't see much blue hair anymore. Maybe in Scottsdale or Miami Beach, but not much even there. Now days when I think of blue hair, I think of Marge Simpson. On her it looks almost natural. Sure, she's a cartoon and she's supposed to stand out, be colorful, but you hardly notice her hair.

On Marge it looks good. Not everyone can pull that off.

The blue hair thing that is, especially when it's teamed up with the yellow skin. What is that? Hepatitis, jaundice or something more sinister, like she's an alien or something. I'm not being critical or racist here when I bring up her yellow skin. Asian people are called the yellow race, but they've never looked yellow to me. Still, I think they had it first. They're kinda like black people who aren't really black and white people who really aren't white. Even white people come in a lot of hues just like everyone else. I think Native Americans have claimed red and

Latinos brown. Green and blue are still up for grabs as far as I know. Truth is, we come in a lot of colors so I guess Marge's yellow hue isn't that hard to accept once you get used to it.

I like it when Marge calls her husband Homer, Homie. It's kinda cute and you can tell she loves the goofy, yellow, bald guy. She has much in common with Edith Bunker, Jill Taylor and too many other television mothers to mention. Challenged by their husbands shortcomings, these women hold their families together in spite of continued frustration and diminished expectations, sometimes for several seasons.

Marge is the voice of reason crying out to her family but often going unheard. Lisa can commiserate with her, being trapped in the same hell of Homer and Bart's making, but Lisa turns inward to her saxophone in times of trouble. Music is her escape. Intellectually, Lisa and Marge are in two very different places. Marge must rely on inner strength to survive the trials of being a Simpson. Occasionally, when she is brought beyond the edge of reason by the boys, Marge can wig out.

Like most women.

Hope springs eternal from the female breast and Marge is no different from any other woman. She loves her family and wants the best for them. Marge doesn't work outside the home just like her predecessors, June Cleaver and Harriet Nelson. She's an old fashioned girl and her place is at home with Maggie, the perpetual infant. Any experiences Marge has had with the workplace have ended disastrously, leading to her conviction that her place was at home.

She can be a little high strung sometimes. Who wouldn't be living with that bunch. When she loses it, she always comes back, a pillar of stability for her family. Not an easy thing to do at the Simpson house where idiotic drama knows no bounds. Whether Homer is interacting with his boss, the wealthy skinflint, old Mr. Burns, or his idealistic, soft spoken neighbor, Ned Flanders, he can be counted on to say just the wrong thing.

Bart should be on some prescription drugs he hasn't bought on the playground. In spite of Bart's sociopathic behavior, Marge loves him, he's her own flesh and blood. She can do nothing else. He may be a juvenile delinquent extraordinaire, but he's her juvenile delinquent. Marge sees the little frightened boy Bart desperately tries to conceal with his tough kid facade. She's the only one who does, but she sees right through Bart. She can't turn her back on her first born in spite of all his shortcomings. Bart makes his cartoon predecessor, Dennis the Menace, look like a choir boy. Dennis' parents however, took a more conventional view of parenting than Marge and Homer.

Lisa was born to play the blues. Highly intelligent and chronically depressed with her inescapable situation, she plays her sax for escape. Lisa is a vegetarian and eventually becomes a Buddhist. Marge is perplexed by Lisa. Far and away the most intelligent of the family, Lisa clings to humanitarian causes like Green Peace to get her through the night. Allegedly only seven years old, Lisa is old beyond her years.

Baby Maggie is coming to grips with the reality into which she's been born. Maggie may be the brightest of the whole bunch. On one episode she spells out

Einstein's theory of relativity ($E = MC^2$) with her blocks, on another she saves Homer's life. Maggie always has a pacifier in her mouth to hide behind, her eyes peering over it at the insanity surrounding her. It's her trademark and it fits her well. Maggie's biggest challenge in life is learning to walk. Most attempts, she lands on her face.

Patty and Selma, Marge's chain smoking, cynical sisters don't like Homer and make no secret about it. They treat him with derision and seize every opportunity to point out his faults and shortcomings to Marge. It falls on deaf ears for Marge writes it off to jealousy. In her eyes, Homer was quite a catch, a football hero with a full head of hair and a job when they fell in love. She knew she could do worse and she admired his predictability. Her Homie's, "Gee, shucks," foot scraping routine melts her heart every time. Homer loves Marge as much as she loves him.

Being a television cartoon mom has its advantages. You might be typecast, but you never really have to worry about work when the show's had its run. Marge has starred in the longest running sit-com, *The Simpsons*, in American history. In addition, *The Simpsons* is the longest running animated and primetime entertainment program of all time.

The Simpsons bridged the millennium and there's no telling where they'll take us. The Marge of the twenty-first century is not that much different from the Marge of the twentieth. Her hair is still blue and her skin yellow. Bart is still a handful, Lisa introspective and baby Maggie is still sucking on her pacifier and falling on her face. Homer...well, Homer is still Homer.

Nothing much changes in Marge's life and she likes it that way.

Harriet Nelson
David and Ricky's Mom

In the 1950's, Harriet Nelson was unique among television moms. She and her husband Ozzie along with their two sons David and Eric (known as Ricky) portrayed themselves every week on *The Adventures of Ozzie and Harriet* starting in October of 1952. The television show was preceded by a radio show of the same name that ran from 1944 until 1954, overlapping the television series by two years.

They, and their neighbor Thorny dealt with all the normal problems associated with suburban life in the fifties. The outdoor scenes were filmed at their actual home and the interior shots were done on a soundstage that reproduced their home. This was nascent, squeaky clean American television. There was no discussion of teenage pregnancy, abortion or homosexuality in the Nelson household. They stuck to topics like counseling the boys on problems with girls and learning to drive. As parents, both Ozzie and Harriet displayed infinite patience and wisdom no matter the situation.

Harriet kept a squeaky clean home in spite of the fact that Ozzie was always around. Apparently he had nowhere to go and was generally available to dispense low key fatherly advice on nearly any subject to anyone who asked. During the entire run of the television show, Ozzie never once went to work, nor was there ever any mention of his occupation or source of income. In the film, *Here Comes the Nelsons* that preceded the television show, he sold women's lingerie. It was the only time his screen alter ego ever held a job. Maybe Harriet thought it was smarter to keep him around the house than selling stockings door to door.

Harriet was attractive, she had sung with Ozzie's big band, performed on radio and in films before turning to television. She and Ozzie married in 1935 when she was performing as the vocalist for his orchestra. Her son David was born on October 24, 1938 and Ricky on May 8, 1940. America witnessed Harriet raising the two boys on radio and television. She set a fine example of American morals and values in the fifties. Ricky, beginning in 1957, regularly performed on the show portraying himself and singing a new song to make the girls all swoon. His first album, *Ricky*, went straight to number one on the Billboard charts. The single, *Poor Little Fool*, went to number one in 1959. Harriet couldn't have been prouder of Ricky having been a singer herself as a young woman. She could often be seen beaming when Ricky performed on the show.

She was about the coolest mom you could have. Harriet might get upset at the boys, but she never raised her voice. Like June Cleaver and the rest of the fifties TV moms, she was always dressed impeccably, and her hair looked like she had just left the beauty parlor. She was a role model for the mothers of the fifties and there were record numbers of them tuning in to watch the Nelson family.

Harriet didn't court controversy. What you saw was what you got. Very little upset her, but you have to remember her sons, David and Ricky were seen by millions of U.S. teens coming of age in the Eisenhower years. Harriet was a gentle, loving mother to them both. She was particularly fond of her youngest, Ricky, but didn't play favorites and left discipline to the easygoing Ozzie when she thought it was required.

Harriet wasn't sexy. She was pretty, vivacious and seldom without a smile on her face, but she wasn't sexy. The fifties weren't about sex, sex wasn't revived in popular entertainment until the sixties. It was hinted at before that and we suspected it was lurking just beneath the surface, but no one really talked about it.

She and Ozzie slept in separate beds. They, like most television couples of that era, owned a set of twin beds. Ward and June Cleaver slept in twin beds. So did Ricky and Lucy. It's amazing that any of these people reproduced. My parents didn't sleep in twin beds and I don't think there were too many others that did either.

The baby boom wasn't the result of every married couple in the United States owning twin beds. When we watched the turtle necked, sanitized version of married America on television, we knew it wasn't reflective of reality. By the time we got to the mid-sixties and reliable birth control, the suppression had created a society in rebellion from repression.

When the boys got older, they married June Blair and Kristin Harmon. Harriet welcomed her daughter-in-laws to the family. She had finally reached the point in her life where she was ready to be a grandmother and we were happy for her. After all, she deserved it. This may have been the first reality TV show and it had lasted for fourteen years.

By 1966, Ozzie and Harriet were an anachronism from the fifties and the show ended. The little morality plays that had become the lifeblood of network television didn't work as well anymore and after years in the public eye, the show was cancelled and the Nelson family walked out of our lives.

I didn't miss them at first. I like many other Americans had moved on to other things. We had grown up with the Nelsons, but were living in a different America. Rick Nelson, as he preferred to be called by 1966, was associated with Elvis and the new record buying teens, the

Boomers, were listening to the Beatles, Stones and Jefferson Airplane.

Harriet still looked good though, and we loved her. I felt affectionate towards her, almost as if she were family. I'd occasionally see her on a talk show. It felt like I was catching up with a favorite aunt I hadn't seen in a long time. I felt bad for her when Ozzie passed away and Ricky died in a plane crash. David, the oldest son, took care of her after that, but she never recovered from her loss. She grieved them both until the day she died.

Ozzie and Harriet will be passing into history before long. Popular entertainment historians and archivists may be familiar with her in years to come, but few young people have ever heard of them. In my mind, Harriet will always smile that bigger than life, motherly smile as she looked proudly at her two sons and loving husband.

She couldn't help herself.

Marie Cunningham
Happy Days Here Again?

Marion Ross played Marion Cunningham, Richie's mom, on *Happy Days* from 1974 to 1984. Like most television mother's on shows set in the fifties, she was a homemaker. Her husband, the easy going Howard, owns a hardware store. Even though the series began filming in the seventies, Marion's children had more in common with the Nelson or Cleaver children than the Roseanne Conner brood. Richie's sister, Joanie doesn't present any more parental challenges than he does. These are essentially clean cut, good kids that don't give their parents a lot of trouble.

Richie can always be counted on to do the right thing. If he has a character flaw, it's his constant quest to meet girls. He's willing to do almost anything to get next to a girl early in the show's run. Later in the series, he finally settles down with a girlfriend, Lori Beth. This stops Richie's constant horndoging and gave the writer's something new to work with, his relationship. Marion, of course, is pleased that her son might finally leave his philandering behind for the stability of Lori Beth and the promise of marriage and grandchildren.

What happened to Chuck?

I'd like to know what happened to Chuck. Chuck Cunningham was Marion's oldest son. He didn't make it past the second season before disappearing. The Fonz's role was being expanded and quite frankly, there wasn't room in the story line for Chuck any more. It was time for Chuck to put on his big boy pants and move on with his life. There was no future for him on *Happy Days*.

Marion never spoke of Chuck again, neither did anyone else on the show. Everyone knew any one of them could be written out of the show next. It was amazing how quickly one could go from starring in a smash hit television show to looking for a dishwashing job on Santa Monica Boulevard. The cover story was that he had moved to Cincinnati or Bangladesh or something. Nobody much cared about Chuck. There wasn't a huge upwelling of protest when he disappeared from the storyline.

It was like he was dead. Some people in the know say he went into the Federal Witness Protection Plan. No one ever saw him again. He's never been seen on a reunion show and no one ever mentioned Chuck in conversation. He's probably running a Seven-Eleven in Boise...or something.

It's kinda strange when you think about it. Based on everything else, Marion is a great mom to her children. Why does she just abandon her first born? Maybe Howard was behind it. He was always suspicious that Chuck was really the mailman's son. He didn't have any hard evidence, just a hunch that something wasn't right. He saw the way Marion and the mailman joked and carried on together. Howard is short and pudgy, but not stupid. Not particularly handsome, Howard isn't bad looking either, but he's no Chuck. One thing he's right about is that Chuck didn't look anything like him.

I guess only Mrs. C knows for sure.

Most of the show's conflict originates outside the Cunningham family. Richie friends, Ralph and Potsie can be counted on to provide some of the drama that the Cunningham's lives would lack without them. As the series progressed, what had been a minor character earlier, Arthur "The Fonz" Fonzerelli took on a larger role.

The Fonz took Chuck's place in Marion's affections when her oldest son disappeared. They have a strange relationship. He calls her Mrs. C and she is the only one who dares to call the Fonz by his real name, Arthur. She's very defensive of Arthur, the way she would be with a child of her own. Is the Fonz a Chuck substitute? Is he the son she never had?

What's the deal with the Fonz? Doesn't he have a mother of his own? He's got a nephew, Chachi (What kind of name is that anyway?) so why doesn't he have a mother? In fact, other than Chachi, he doesn't seem to have any relatives.

During the course of the show, we learn that Arthur and his mother were abandoned by his father. Somehow, he becomes estranged from his mother. She shows up as a mysterious stranger at

Arnold's diner in one episode. She denies being the Fonz's mother, but a picture in her wallet of the young Fonz reveals the truth.

Eventually, the Fonz moves into the bachelor pad above the Cunningham's garage. This opens up all kinds of possibilities. Considering Howard's past suspicions and Marion's overt affection for the Fonz, it makes you wonder whether Howard has any common sense. It's kinda like having the pool boy, Raul, move in after you've caught your wife watching him from the kitchen window.

Not the best idea in the world.

There's probably nothing going on anyhow. Marion is pretty, but she buys her dresses at the same place June and Harriet shop. Her clothes are not revealing or provocative. She doesn't exactly exude sexuality, but then again she's not supposed to be sexy. After all, she's a fifties mom.

No one is even sure how women got pregnant back then. What with the long dresses that covered them from ankle to neck you needed quite an imagination to picture them naked. They didn't even sleep with their husbands. A lot of them even slept in separate rooms. It's hard to imagine how they became pregnant in the sexless television world of twin beds they inhabited. Still, they did manage to reproduce even though it must have been a difficult and surreptitious undertaking.

It's even harder to imagine Howard naked. Maybe at some time in his life, Howie was buff, but it must have been a long time before we met him. It's not that he was repulsive or anything, but it's like imagining your parents having sex.

You just don't want to think about it.

Imagine naked Howard chasing Marion through the house, while the kids are at the zoo with the church group. She's slow in heels and even Howard with his Pillsbury Dough Boy physique manages to run her down.

Not pretty is it?

Movie Mothers

Most television mothers are tame compared to movie moms. That's strange considering they usually only have two hours to develop the character and create an impression. That's not always easy. They can get away with more in the movies than they can on television. I think that's good. Seeing Nicole Kidman in the nude is one thing, seeing Roseanne Barr as Roseanne, is quite another. There needs to be limits to what we're expected to endure on television.

That's why we go to the movies.

The best movie moms are unforgettable. Faye Dunaway's portrayal of Joan Crawford in *Mommy Dearest* stands out among the mommy movies. Mama Corleone of the *Godfather* trilogy was a special kind of mother to a very unique family. In *E.T. the Extra Terrestrial*, Mary, the mother of Elliot who rescues E.T., is pretty much oblivious to the fact she has an alien living in her kid's closet.

Best to look in there every once in a while I guess. You never know what you'll find.

In *Titanic*, Rose's mother, Ruth Bukater is willing to sell her daughter out to the evil Cal Hockley, if it will help her maintain her current standard of living. When Rose questions the arrangement, her mother accuses her of being selfish.

In *Scarface*, Madre Montana is a woman of principals. When her son Tony resurfaces in her life, she tries in vain to get rid of him before he can influence her daughter, the innocent Gina. Tony bankrolls his little sister's new lifestyle, and it isn't long before she's doing cocaine and having sex in nightclub bathrooms.

Of all the movie moms in film history, the scariest had to be Anthony Perkins' mom in *Psycho*. Norman Bates, proprietor of the Bate's Motel conducts a constant dialogue with his long dead mother. You only get a glimpse of her mummified body in the film, but it's enough to make your hair stand on end.

Mother Bates is tough, but she only has Norman's best interests at heart...or does he?

Movie moms grab us. Everyone has a mother, so it's easy to relate to these bigger than life mothers who appear on the screen. In *Sophie's Choice*, Meryl Streep plays concentration camp survivor, Sophie Zawistowski who is emotionally crippled from making a choice no mother should have to make.

The one thing movie moms are not is dull.

Joan Crawford
Mommy Dearest

This is one unique movie in that not only is the mother, Joan Crawford, a real mother, but the story is told from her adopted daughter, Christine Crawford's, perspective. Joan has to be the worst movie mother of all time. Granted, she has some mental problems, but the woman shouldn't be raising children. She shouldn't even be around them.

Joan Crawford miscarried seven times before turning to adoption. Conventional adoption agencies turned her down because of her age and celebrity lifestyle. In the film, her fictional boyfriend, Hollywood attorney, Greg Savitt, arranges for her to adopt her first child, Christine. It's a tender moment when adoptive mother, Joan and baby Christine first meet, but things rapidly go downhill from there as Crawford's mental condition deteriorates. Christine isn't very old when she begins to realize that "Mommy Dearest," as Joan requires her to address her, might not be quite right. As a mother, Joan continually reinforces Christine's belief throughout her childhood.

Joan throws a lavish birthday party for Christine that is well attended by the children of Hollywood's elite. That evening, Crawford gives Christine her personal birthday present, a beautiful doll. Joan asks the girl to pick her favorite birthday present and Christine wisely chooses the doll. This pleases Joan who tells her she can keep the doll but the rest of her presents will be donated to charity to be given to less fortunate little girls. She even arranged a photo op with Christine for the press. Christine is upset, but she knows better than to challenge her mother.

As the movie progresses, we begin to get the feeling that Joan has adopted children for the publicity opportunities they present. Near the end of the movie, she admits to Christine that publicity may have had some bearing on her decision to adopt. The viewer suspects it may have played a much more important role.

Few of us think of our children as photo ops.

Alcohol fuels a lot of Joan's behavior. She's never far from a bottle and when she is, she has the pocket flask given to her by Cuban dictator, Batista. Vanity plays a part, too. Her brutal beauty regimen as depicted in the opening scenes of the movie began at 4:00 AM each day. As she aged, her efforts became more and more desperate. She became obsessed, convinced that if she could only hold on to her youthful appearance, her career and future would be assured.

In spite of her best efforts, she failed.

When the theaters dubbed her, "Box Office Poison," Louis B. Mayer released her from her contract. Her firing did nothing to improve her mental condition and inspired her to drink even more than usual. This leads her, dressed in a ball gown, to destroy her prized rose garden in the middle of the night. Wielding pruning shears to take out her frustrations, Joan rousts the children from bed to make them participate in the destruction. When she instructs Christine to bring her the ax from the garden shed, Christine exchanges an alarmed glance with her young brother.

Luckily, Joan only has plans to chop down an offensive ornamental tree.

In the infamous coat hanger scene, Joan has a psychotic episode late one night while wandering the house, her face painted white with cream and a drink in her hand. Going through her daughter's closet she discovers a dress hanging on a wire coat hanger and proceeds to come unglued. Waking an eight year old Christina to rave at her about the importance of not using wire coat hangers, she then proceeds to completely trash the girl's bedroom and bathroom. She caps it off by beating the girl with the offending hanger. When she finally regains her senses, she screams at the girl to clean her filthy room.

Not long after, Christine is sitting at her mother's makeup table playing the way little girls will do. Joan walks up behind her and doesn't like what she sees. Interpreting her daughter's play as the child ridiculing her, she becomes irrational and hacks a weeping Christine's hair off with a pair of shears to teach her a lesson about vanity, humility and irrational behavior.

When Joan finally tires of Christina, she does what many wealthy parents do when they have had enough of parenthood, and sends her off to a convent boarding school for troublesome children. In spite of her initial misgivings, Christine thrives there. It turns out that the severe, black clad nuns, present a welcome relief from Mommy Dearest. It's a sad day and many tears are shed when Christine says goodbye to the Mother Superior and leaves the convent school to return to the loving arms of mother Joan..

When an older Christine defies her, Joan flies into a rage, attacks her and knocks her to the floor. Straddling her, she begins choking her and beating her head against the marble floor.   Joan's personal assistant finally pulls her off Christine before she can kill her. This all occurs while a journalist from Redbook magazine is there to do a feature piece on her.

I can just imagine that article.

As an adult, Christine suffers from a benign ovarian tumor, is hospitalized and unable to continue in her soap opera role. Luckily, Mommy Dearest is prepared to step in and somehow convinces the show's director to let her fill in while Christine convalesces. The fact that Joan is at least thirty years older than Christine's character doesn't seem to faze anyone. Joan's drinking hampers her performance, but no one cares much. When Christine recovers, she resumes her role.

The movie deviates significantly from real life in its omission of Crawford's other two adopted daughters, Cindy and Cathy. The two youngest of the Crawford siblings repudiated Christine's book on which the movie was based. As a result, neither of them were portrayed, or even mentioned, in the movie. Christine's younger brother, Christopher is spared his sister's abuse as portrayed in the movie, but in real life he suffered at the hands of his mother, as much, if not more than she.

Joan Crawford died of cancer in 1977. In the end, reaching out to her children from the grave to slap them one last time, she leaves them nothing in her will. but Christine has her revenge when she publishes her memoir, *Mommy Dearest,* in 1978.

Mama Corleone
She Seems So Nice

Family was everything to the Corleones. At least when they weren't trying to kill each other or everyone around them. Fredo tried to kill his brother Michael and failed. Later Fredo said he didn't mean it. There had been a mistake of some kind and he had lost a great deal of sleep over the incident. Michael didn't kill Fredo immediately, but like a good son and out of respect for his mother, he waited until after she had passed away to dispatch his brother.

Things hadn't always been this way for Carmela Corleone. She started out life as the wife of an honest Italian immigrant living in a New York tenement. She could barely speak English when she was married to Robert DeNiro in the second movie which took place before the first movie but before the third and after the first.

Got that?

Things start to get interesting when her husband Vito, loses his job at the

161

grocery to make room for the local crime boss' nephew. Vito helps out one of the neighborhood aspiring thugs by hiding a gun and is rewarded with a rug they steal from an uptown brownstone. When he brings the rug home, Mama doesn't ask too many questions, she just puts the infant Sonny down on it to play.

She doesn't have much of a role in the first movie. Sure, she dances at the wedding and the Don hears her crying after Sonny's assassination while he is recovering from an attempt on his own life, but there's nothing deep. We have to wait until the second movie when she has a bigger role before she starts dispensing any advice.

With the Godfather gone, Michael has no one to turn to but his mother. Disturbed by the disintegration of the extended Corleone family and a strong desire to murder his older brother Fredo, Michael joins his mother by the fireside. Carmela assures Michael that he can never lose his family, but Michael's not so sure about that. People are dropping like flies around him and so far he's been lucky, but he knows it's just a matter of time before his luck runs out. Mama Corleone appears to be oblivious to what's going on and she doesn't ask where all the money comes from.

Does she really think the olive oil business is that good?

How could it be? Her husband, Don Vito Corleone, is the most feared dealer of olive oil on Long Island. They live in a big house with a wall around the courtyard. There's always a lot of guys around with guns. People you've known for years, suddenly disappear. Her husband is always running around negotiating with people and making them lucrative offers they almost always accept.

How Mama Corleone doesn't notice all this going on around her is anyone's guess. Her son is turned into hamburger at a toll booth and someone tries to do the same to her husband on the streets of Little Italy in Manhattan. The olive oil business has really gotten competitive on the east coast from all appearances.

She's got to have a clue what's going on around her. In the beginning, when she is a young mother, struggling and destitute, it's easier to overlook the occasional rug or dress. When you find yourself living in a fortress manned by your husband's private army, you'd think you'd be a little curious.

How do we afford a private army importing olive oil?

She never asks the question though. It seems like it would be tough to ignore. Women weren't encouraged to ask questions about their husband's business back then. She enforced the no business talk at the dinner table. She was one of the few who could correct or discipline the headstrong Sonny, her oldest son.

Sonny is a brute. He was a brute as a little boy. As a man, he is vicious and speaks in anger without thinking, much to his father's disappointment. Sonny has a family, but they're kept in the background. At his sister's wedding, Sonny takes a bridesmaid upstairs for some extra-marital activities. Sonny might be just a little psychotic, but he is Carmela's psycho and she loves him.

Fredo is everyone's disappointment. The godfather passes him over for Don in favor of Michael. Miffed by the slight, Fredo pursues the fast life in Las Vegas and Havana. Sickly as a child, Carmella has a soft spot for him as an adult. In spite of the fact that he wasn't as tough as Sonny or smart as Michael, Carmela loves her maladjusted, frail Fredo.

Michael, the son and war hero who rejected the family business, denouncing it to his sweetheart Kay, takes over the crime empire as soon as his father begins to fail. Michael is smarter and more viscous than Don Vito, but in the end still loses everything that matters to him.

Connie, Carmela's only daughter is a head case after Michael orders her husband Carlo murdered for his role in the shooting of Don Vito. She runs from man to man, drinks too much and lives off the family. Mama is not pleased with her daughter and is even less impressed with her latest fiancé, a hapless WASP himbo sniffing around for a meal ticket.

In addition to her natural children, she is also the adoptive mother of Tom Hagen, a German/Irish orphan Sonny brought home from the streets as a boy. She raises Tom as her own and he is treated as an equal even though he is occasionally reminded by his step-brothers that he is neither blood or Sicilian. Much to his credit, he sticks up for himself, even to Sonny.

Mama Corleone is a pious woman. She prays for her husband and children's souls every day. She's worried they're not going to make it to heaven where she hopes to be waiting for them with her husband Vito.

My guess is she's going to be waiting a long time if she even makes it herself. That ignorance plea isn't going to work with the big guy. At the very least there's that guilt by association thing. Carmela Soprano at least has no false pretenses regarding what Tony does for a living. She commiserates with the other mob wives, but they all know what their husbands do for a living down at the Bada Bing. They know about the gombas and can guess about the rest. These women, like Mama Corleone, have grown accustomed to the comfortable lifestyles they lead and don't care that it's financed by organized crime. Carmela Soprano enjoys the beach house and the status of being Tony's wife.

She knows where the money is hidden.

Mama Corleone, doesn't know where the money is hidden and doesn't care. All her needs are taken care of while spending her golden years at Michael's estate on Lake Tahoe. Sure there's the occasional shootings and crooked politicians to deal with there, but it's got a great view and it's infinitely better than Jersey.

Madre Scarface
Even Tony Had a Mother

Tony Montana pulls up in front of his mother's modest home on the edge of the refinery district outside Miami and he sees it as a triumphal return. He's being driven in a twenty year old yellow Cadillac convertible with leopard skin upholstery that looks like new. At that time in Miami, or at least Havana, this was a sure sign that you had made it.

When he shows up at Georgina's door after an absence of five years, his mother is almost civil at first, but she blocks the door, refusing to let her own son into the house. When Tony's sister comes to the door to see who's there, she reluctantly allows him in the house.

While Gina is thrilled to see her older brother again, Mama Georgina doesn't look happy to see her first born, barely containing her anger at his presence. Georgina isn't just disappointed in Tony, she really doesn't like him and she is regretting that she let him in her home.

When she does, the pot begins to boil and it isn't long before it explodes.

Sitting at their modest kitchen table, Gina begins to fill Tony in on their lives and her ambitions to become a hair stylist. Mama stands off to the side, her arms folded across her chest, glaring at Tony, wanting him to disappear again from their simple but honest lives. As Gina goes on about her plans for the future, Tony interrupts her.

"All that's over!" Tony says triumphantly.

In a generous gesture, Tony takes $1,000 from his pocket and offers it to his mother, but she refuses to touch the money, knowing in her heart that it is blood money.

"Who did you kill for that?" she demands.

"No one," says Tony. "Your son's made it."

"Son? I wish I had a son," she retorts.

Tony contends that he's working for an anti-Castro group and the money he's offering her comes from "donations." Tony is stammering because even he can't buy that line and Georgina explodes. She throws his money at him and tells him to leave. She blocks the door so Gina can't go to him. Tony's no fool, and he doesn't have too much pride to gather the money up from the floor. His mother tells him that people like him give Cubans a bad name as he picks up the cash.

His mother screams at him, "I work for my living," as he leaves.

Gina, upset by the scene between Tony and her mother, pushes past her and runs outside after him. He hugs his baby sister and she says to him, "You're my blood, always." It's the most tender moment in the film, maybe the only one in an exceedingly violent film.

Tony gives her the cash, tells her to go out and have some fun and buy something for the old lady with the attitude inside the house. In spite of his mother's flat out rejection, he still wants her to have something. Whether it is a testament to Georgina's skill as a mother or Cuban culture is undetermined. Later in the film, when the cocaine business is really good, he buys Gina a beauty salon in a five star neighborhood and a tiger for himself.

Crazy some of the things people will spend money on.

When Tony's mom says she doesn't want anything to do with him she means it. We never see her in the movie again after the reunion scene. Gina continues to evolve with the story, but Mother Montana disappears from the story never to return. Guess she wasn't kidding when she said she didn't want anything to do with him.

Later in the story, Gina has no problem accepting the fruits of Tony's ill gotten gains. She is now delighted to be eating in fine restaurants and nightclubs. She gets used to dressing in designer gowns, not the Wal-Mart couture she had been accustomed to wearing before her brother came back into her life. Then there's the added benefit of having all the cocaine she can snort, which helps her stay runway thin. That seems to work out well for everyone in the story including Tony. There's nothing like a life time supply of cocaine to help you wile away the years.

Meanwhile, back in the low rent district by the refineries, what's Mom doing? Renting out Gina's room to pick up a little cash? Georgina is obviously a principled woman. Unlike Mama Corleone, Tony's mother Georgina wasn't in denial, she knew exactly what she had brought into the world and regretted her contribution to organized crime. This is one strong woman. No one else gets away with talking to Tony the way she does. She's intimidating enough that Tony knows better than to argue with her.

Only she calls him, "Antonio."

Georgina has chosen her pride and principals over an easy life that required her to overlook her son's business dealings. She has her little house and job at the factory. It only provides a modest living, but she can hold her head high and sleeps well at night when she's not worrying about Gina. Even when Tony marries his former boss' widow, Elvira (Michelle Pfeiffer), Mama Montana is nowhere to be seen among the guests.

Maybe she couldn't make up her mind between the chicken and the fish.

I know one thing, Mama Montana should have washed young Antonio's mouth out with soap. He has the foulest mouth in movie history. He uses the all purpose F word in almost every sentence, sometimes twice, even three times. His imagination for fitting it into a sentence knows no bounds.. Sometimes it's a noun, other times a verb or an adjective. It's almost like Tony's all purpose word.

His friend Manny doesn't talk like that, only Tony does. The other tough guys don't use the word as much as Tony. They seem just as dangerous as he does, but they don't have to use that language. They find it kind of embarrassing, almost as if he were ignorant or something. Somebody should talk to him about his language, but everyone is afraid of the guy with a tiger for a pet. Eventually, he ends up killing just about everyone in the movie but his mother.

Guess she was right about him all along.

E.T.'s Foster Mom
Not to Worry

In the movie *E.T. The Extra Terrestrial*, Dee Wallace portrays Mary, a young single mother with an alien living in her son's closet. She doesn't know it at first, which is just as well, because she's just barely coping with life. Recently separated from her husband, she is not taking to single motherhood well and neither are her three children, Michael, Elliot and little Gertie. When they mention Dad is in Mexico with his new girlfriend, she breaks into tears. She makes remarks regarding Mexico and her soon-to-be ex for the remainder of the movie.

The family lives in a nice California neighborhood and Mary dresses for work, but it's unclear what she does for a living. Money doesn't seem to be an issue like it does for many fractured families. She's driving a new Audi and the family doesn't seem to want for anything other than her husband's, the kid's father, presence.

When Elliot adopts an abandoned alien he discovers in their shed, things start to get interesting. Baiting his new friend with Reese's Pieces, Elliot gets E.T. off the streets and to the temporary refuge of his bedroom. The next morning, Elliot fakes being sick and Mary believes him, giving him the day off school to play with the new friend he's hidden in his closet.

When Mom comes in the bedroom, E.T. retreats to the closet where he comingles with a bunch of stuffed animals. Mary opens the closet door, but doesn't connect the new stuffed animal with an alien life form. Short, squat and green, E.T. fits right in with the rest of the fuzzy creatures.

In spite of several close encounters, Mary never really comes face to face with E.T. until the last part of the film. When she finally meets her house guest, she stays calm and gets Elliot and Gertie out of the bedroom in spite of their repeated protestations that E.T. is harmless.

You've got to admire this woman. She finds an extra-terrestrial camped out in her house and by all appearances, he's her kid's new best friend. Yet, she stays calm, this woman doesn't get hysterical, she takes care of business. It takes a lot of talking to convince her that E.T. is harmless, but she's willing to listen to her kids, even little Gertie (played adoringly by six year old Drew Barrymore in her second film appearance).

Considering the subject matter of this film, Mary is an exemplary movie mom, not even a hint of feminine panic or hysteria that you would expect from a stereotype when she finds an alien in the house. She's not funny or desperate, but that's okay, she's something better...she's believable. You can't help but like her. She's fair when she doles out punishment and she doesn't jump to conclusions or overreact.

She loves her kids and her kids love her, that is apparent.

What's more, Dee Wallace who portrays Mary, does a great job creating a sympathetic, believable character. Life isn't easy for Mary but she doesn't wallow in self-pity. She does the only thing she knows how to do, she keeps on keeping on.

It's not always easy. She breaks out in tears when the kids mention their father, his new girlfriend or Mexico where the former are vacationing. The closest she comes to an invective is when she says, "He doesn't even like Mexico!"

There is no temper tantrum or emotional outburst, only a little justifiable pouting.

Mary allows herself a moment of righteous anger and a few tears, but she quickly recovers and goes back to being Mom. She's handling a full time responsible position at work and raising three children including a very young and precocious, Gertie. Into this mix is thrown an abandoned alien followed closely by the federal authorities who commander her home in an effort to isolate and examine E.T. and Elliot, both of whom appear to be dying.

When Mary has to tell Gertie that E.T. is dying, she does it gently, comforting her with words a child could understand and accept. When Elliot begins to recover as E.T. dies, she is relieved and mourns E.T.'s passing with her children. Somehow, Mary understands the significance the gentle alien's presence has had in their lives.

When E.T. is reborn in an amazing reincarnation, she stands back and lets her kids plan and execute his escape. She figures she's got nothing left to lose at this point. They've wrapped her house up in some kind of heavy duty government Saran Wrap, there are cables and people everywhere invading her space and they've turned her living room into an ICU. By the time this all plays out, she's probably going to lose the kids for harboring an extra-terrestrial fugitive.

All of this in spite of her talking to the kids about bringing home strays...from anywhere.

In the end, she and the government agent, catch up with the kids and E.T. at the clearing in the forest where E.T.s rescue ship is waiting for him. Considering the circumstances, everyone is pretty relaxed. There's a large alien spacecraft sitting there in front of them, but no one is overreacting. There is no hysteria even though it could easily be forgiven.

All things considered, she's pretty cool about all this. I don't know if I could sit and watch my kid saying tearful goodbyes to his alien buddy without being a little anxious. I mean we've all heard about those experiments they do on abducted humans.   If you are unaware of this problem, all I can say is you need to get to the grocery store and check out the latest *Enquirer* while you're waiting in line.

I'd be concerned Elliot would be going along for the ride with his new buddy, never to be seen again.   Luckily, E.T. only takes the potted begonias with him when he walks up the ramp to the alien spacecraft.   When the aliens take off, Mary and the family watch the craft soar across the sky leaving a rainbow in its trail.   You almost hope that nice government agent and her will hook up and she can finally leave her ex behind.

I mean, now that the alien thing is over.

Rose's Titanic Mama
Champagne Tastes...

Ruth Dewitt Bukater was a miserable mother. In spite of her upper class airs and ambitions for her daughter Rose, she was destitute. The late Mr. Bukater left them nothing but debt when he died. This unforeseen turn of events was disturbing to a woman so much better than her peers. In Rose, she saw her last opportunity to maintain an upper class lifestyle for herself in spite of having nothing left but the appearance of wealth and a snobbish attitude. She sees the marriage of her seventeen year old daughter to the arrogant Cal Hockley as more of a business arrangement than a love match...a very lucrative business arrangement.

At this point you might be asking yourself, "Who are these people?"

Does a big ship and even bigger iceberg ring a bell? Rose Bukater is the pivotal character in the 1997 motion picture *Titanic*. Ruth, her mother, will stop at nothing to marry her daughter to Cal, the son and heir of a Pittsburg steel magnate. Cal has promised to pay off their substantial debt in order to secure the reluctant Rose as his wife.

Ruth is anxious to make this happen in spite of the fact that Rose is clearly not interested in Cal or a lifetime of dinner parties and idle chatter. She explains to Rose that she is being selfish and that marriage to Cal will secure both their futures, but Rose isn't buying it, not even a little bit. Ruth clearly does not understand the importance her daughter places on love or the fact that Rose doesn't love Cal and never will.

Ruth is a snob's snob. For company, she prefers royalty. If there's none available, a Vanderbilt or Astor will do. Molly Brown's money was much too fresh to pass muster with Ruth and her friends. In one scene, Ruth and company try to avoid her on deck by getting up from their seats when she sits down to join the ladies. Oblivious to their snub, she gets right back up and strolls down the deck with them.

As things unfold, it becomes obvious that Rose has little say in her future. Her mother and Cal conspire to make Rose comply with their wishes. Cal shows her a huge diamond, The Heart of the Ocean and says it will be hers when they marry. He suggests he could give her anything she pleases and declares, "We're royalty." He implies that a little pre-marital loving might be an appropriate response to his generous gift.

Rose has other thoughts and passes on his booty call. Cal isn't pleased by her rejection.

I don't know anyone who has names for their jewelry. I've heard about the Hope Diamond of course and its attendant curse. How big does the diamond have to be before you can give it a name? The Hope diamond weighs about forty-five carats. Of course it's a real diamond, not like the Heart of the Ocean and nobody has thrown it in the Atlantic like in the movie. I've never been big on jewelry. Maybe I'll give my watch a name like Bob or something. Perhaps something more exciting. I'll have to think about it.

Sitting next to her mother and Cal at dinner in the first class dining room on Titanic, Rose begins to sink into despair as she listens to the conversation and realizes that she can't accept it as her future. Bolting from dinner, she makes her way to the stern of the ship where she contemplates and almost commits suicide if not for Jack Dawson. Jack is invited to join their party for dinner the next night as a reward for saving the life of Rose.

He has found a friend in Molly Brown who provides him with a tuxedo and sound advice in dealing with the upper crust. At dinner, Ruth goes out of her way to insult Jack, but he doesn't take her bait. In spite of the fact that Jack has saved Rose's life, Ruth senses their mutual attraction and takes an intense dislike of him.

As we all know, this fun doesn't last long. Rose's attraction to Jack has made Ruth a nervous wreck. In spite of her best efforts, Rose admires Jack even more. The two of them slip away and after a modeling session in Rose's first class suite, make love in the back seat of a luxury car stowed in the hold. Jack is framed for the theft of the Heart of the Ocean and the ship starts to sink.

Somewhere in there they hit an iceberg. I didn't mention it because everybody knows about the iceberg and the Titanic. The iceberg thing is almost incidental to the love story. Jack is there to rescue Rose from a pointless existence with shallow Cal, even if he has to die doing it. The only thing that could make this story any better would be if Ruth were Rose's evil stepmother and there were dwarfs or something.

"Are the lifeboats being seated by class?"

I suppose that's a legitimate question if you're a narrow minded, self absorbed, snob like Ruth. She's even concerned that the lifeboat will be too crowded or have the wrong kind of people on board. It's understandable. For what those tickets cost it better be a first class lifeboat. Rose explains to her mother that there aren't enough lifeboats for everyone and that half the people on board are going to die.

Rose refuses to join her mother in the lifeboat and it is lowered without her. Rose decides to take her chances with the Titanic rather than her mother and jumps back on board. Now Ruth is left on the lifeboat with Molly Brown who doesn't care how important Ruth thinks she is or who she knows. Molly Brown impresses upon Ruth the importance of putting some distance between them and the sinking ship to avoid getting sucked down with the Titanic. As a result there is a good chance that Ruth got some blisters on her dainty hands pulling on those first class oars.

That's the last we see of Ruth. Cal looks for Rose among the third class survivors on the Carpathia, but she turns her back to him, not wishing to be found. Without Rose to bargain for the good life, we assume that Cal loses interest in supporting Ruth pretty quickly, but we don't know what really happens to her once the ship reaches New York. Maybe she ended up dishing out fast food in Times Square or something like that.

Mrs. Bates
Motel Proprietor

Norman Bates is one messed up individual and his mother might be to blame...or maybe not. It's hard to tell because we really don't know where Mother Bates ends and Norman begins. Seems Norman is a little schizophrenic and has been trying to sort things out since his mother died up there in that old house on top of the hill overlooking their ratty motel. He doesn't seem to be that bad a guy when he's Norman, it's Mother Bates you have to be careful around.

When Norman's mother died, he stole her body and mummified it to keep him company. Occasionally he likes to dress up in her clothes but usually only when he's feeling a little kinky. We're not sure, but it almost seems like Mother Bates is inhabiting Norm's body and there's a struggle going on for its possession.

Maybe she's not really dead. Perhaps there's just been a change of address.

Norman conscientiously runs the Bates Motel with his mother as he has for years. He's shy around girls and when he asks new guest and fugitive, Marion Crane, up to the house for dinner, it takes all the courage he can muster. Much to his surprise, Marion accepts his offer, which thrills Norman who leaves and goes up to the house to prepare the meal.

Marion overhears Norman violently arguing with his mother over his dinner invitation. Mother Bates loudly suggests that Norman is only interested in the young woman for sex and Norman screams at her, "Shut up!" A door slams and before long she sees Norman coming down the hill to the motel with a tray of milk and sandwiches. He suggests they eat in the motel office rather than the house and Marion graciously agrees to his suggestion.

During dinner, Marion admits she heard Norman and his mother arguing. Norman tries to minimize the conflict and tells her that his mother became "ill" after the death of his father and complains about being a prisoner sentenced to caring for her. When she suggests that it might be time to move her to a rest home, he becomes agitated and maintains that that is out of the question. Norman maintains that he has always taken care of his mother and always will. Unbeknownst to her, Marion has not only offended Norman, but Mother Bates as well.

At this point, we're not sure if there's a real Mother Bates or not. We've seen her through the window up on the hill, but it wasn't like she was waving or anything, mostly she was just a silhouette in the window. We aren't even aware that the imaginative and talented Norman is doing both voices, his own and his mother's. If Marion knew, it would probably creep her out, but she never discovers Norman's secret.

The dinner date goes badly after that and Marion retreats to her room. She decides that Norman is harmless, unaware that it's his mother that is the true danger. After dinner with Norman, Marion feels an almost compulsive desire to shower. Norman probably does that to all the girls and a lot of the guys when they meet him. As she undresses, Norman observes her through a peephole from the office. That rates about a ten on the creep meter.

Now we all know not to take a shower at the Bates Motel. Unfortunately, no one has told Marion and not long after she gets into the shower, she meets Norman's mother. Or is it just Norman dressed up like his mother? It's hard to tell. Hitchcock did that on purpose to build tension and it worked. One thing we're certain of is that someone has brought a very large knife into the bathroom and begins to stab Marion until she is dead on the shower floor, her lifeblood flowing down the drain.

We get a quick glance at the killer and the flashing knife. It looks like it could be Mother Bates. We haven't had a good look at her previous to the shower scene. Sure, we've seen her up on the hill through the window, but we couldn't pick her out of a line-up. Strangely, she looks a little bit like the actor Anthony Perkins in drag.

Clearly, Mother Bates doesn't want any floozy messing with her good son Norman. Of course, according to Mother Bates, all women are tramps. She is the only woman in Norman's life and she intends to keep it that way...and so does Norman.

When she returns to the house on the hill covered in blood, we hear Norman screaming and we see him come running down the hill to Marion's room. There he is shocked to find his mother's handy work. As usual, Norman is stuck cleaning up his mother's mess. He gathers up all the evidence and Marion's body, stuffs it all in the trunk of Marion's car along with what's left of Marion and sinks it in a pond.

It isn't long before Mother Bates claims another victim when a detective comes nosing around, looking for Marion. He makes the mistake of going in the house uninvited after talking to Norman about Marion's disappearance. The detective climbs the stairs of the old house and when he reaches the top of the stairs, he meets Mother Bates holding a very large knife. She slashes him across the face and pushes him down the steps. Just to make sure he's dead, she follows him down the stairs and continues stabbing the hapless detective. This really makes Norman angry and in spite of her protestations, he throws her over his shoulder and carries her to the basement of the house where she'll be safe and stop knifing people.

When Marion's boyfriend Sam and her sister Lila come looking for her and the missing detective, things really get interesting. While Sam keeps Norman busy at the motel office, Lila sneaks up to the house to look around. Norman gets wise and a scuffle ensues, which leaves Sam on the office floor, unconscious.

When Norman comes in the house, Lila retreats to the basement and meets the real Mother Bates for the first time. While she's reacting to the mommy mummy, Norman in drag shows up with a knife again only to be subdued by a revived Sam.

Later, a psychiatrist tells Lila and Sam that Mother Bates had come to live inside of Norman and the two of them were struggling for control of Norman's body. Confined to a mental institution, Mother finally prevails and Norman becomes just a memory.

Whew.

Gillian Guiler
Too Close an Encounter

Gillian Guiler (Melinda Dillon) has it tough. She's a single mom living with her three year old son, Barry in an old farmhouse outside of Muncie, Indiana. Recently single, she's struggling to make ends meet. She has a lot in common with E.T.'s adopted mom. They're both trying to juggle a career, raise children by themselves and deal with the aliens.

Late one night Barry is awakened by his toys coming to life in his room. Animated by some unknown force, the toys begin to whirl and move of their own accord. Amazed by the activity, Barry sits there amused until he hears a noise downstairs. Too young to be frightened, he makes his way down the stairs and finds the front door wide open and the living room trashed. When he turns towards the kitchen he sees something that makes him smile.

That's about the time Gillian wakes up, her sleep disturbed by the energized toys coming into her room. When she gets up and looks out the window, she sees Barry running across the yard towards the trees. In a panic, she runs outside and chases him across a field to a hillside of saucer watchers. Roy Neary (Richard Dreyfus) almost runs the boy over with his pickup truck as Barry stands in the middle of the road, transfixed by the sky. Gillian snatches him out of the way as Roy hits the guard rail. Uninjured, Roy joins them to see if the boy is hurt.

Before long, small alien ships come flashing down the road with the police in hot pursuit and their attention is diverted. When the police try to keep up with them they predictably drive off the road at high speed. There's no keeping up with these boys in the saucers and they're having a little fun with the local constabulary.

This is Gillian's first hint that something isn't quite right. When she sees the number of saucer watchers in their lawn chairs, she just shakes her head in wonder, relieved that Barry has escaped unscathed. She's not looking at the big picture yet. She's still in the safe little world that she and Barry inhabit in the country. They have their daily travails to put up with, but nothing cosmic has intruded into their lives...until now.

It isn't long before Gillian is wishing she just had problems like the child support check being late. That she could deal with. The aliens trashing her home is starting to grow old. Groceries are expensive and she's not smiling when she sees them strewn across the kitchen, milk in pools and broken eggs littering the floor.

Not long after, the aliens show up again. Gillian is taking the trash out when she notices something strange in the sky. As she stands by the trash barrel her attention is drawn by thunder and a strange, cloud formation. Entranced by the odd sight, she suddenly realizes she's witnessing the return of the aliens. She drops the waste basket and runs to the house where Barry is playing alone.

Another energy surge, stronger than the first, turns on every electrical device in the house and puts them into overload. As she shuts windows and locks doors, an intense light envelopes the house. When her attention is diverted by the beam of light coming down the fireplace chimney,

Barry crawls out the dog door.   Gillian lunges to grab him, but it is too late.

Barry has left with the aliens.

These kind of events would make most mothers come unglued.   It would make most fathers come unglued.   This isn't the kind of thing that the police can easily help you with.   There might be an ad in one of the tabloids for someone who claims they can help, but it's hard to find any really endorsements or actual help. These are not the kind of things most people deal with on a daily basis. I hardly know anyone who claims to have been abducted.

Except for Uncle Bert but that's another story.

Searching for Barry, she is reunited with Roy in a crowd of refugees gathered in a small Wyoming town. Neither of them understands why they have come there and they're not alone.   People from all over the country are being inexplicably drawn to the area only to be turned away by the military.   She and Roy are more determined than the others and he devises a plan to help them satisfy their curiosity.

Now things are getting a little weird for Gillian. First Barry takes off with the aliens. He's not really abducted, he seems more than willing to go with them. Now she's hooked up with this whack job that's more out there than she is. He's the perfect candidate for her partner, he's obsessed. Nothing is going to stop Roy, and right now, that's what Gillian is looking for in a man, someone who will help her find Barry.

Now mind you, neither of them are even certain why they're there. They can't explain any of the strange thoughts that have been filling their heads. Gillian seems calmer than she should be, almost as if she knows that if she's in the right place at the right time, Barry will return to her.

Roy and Gillian take off cross country in his station wagon mowing down roadblocks and fences without a second thought. Their luck finally runs out and they're apprehended by the army and quarantined. They're determined and it isn't long before they escape and make their way up the mountain.

We're not certain why Roy is even there other than the telepathic messages the aliens have been sending him. Gillian is there searching for Barry, but even she doesn't know what has led her to the middle of nowhere in Wyoming from Muncie, Indiana.

It's unclear why they try to climb the mountain. The government has the whole landing strip set up on the other side of Devil's mountain, not in it. I suppose it adds to the drama. Anyhow, while she and Roy hide in the rocks and observe (some security that no one notices them) the scientist's activity, the aliens make an entrance. While she's busily snapping pictures, Roy makes his way down to the crowd that's so engrossed with the alien mother ship that they don't even notice his unauthorized presence.

Another security breach.

Before long, abductees start walking down the ramp from the mother ship, returning home not a day older than the day they were grabbed. It has something to do with the speed of light, but it's way too deep for me.

It's not long before Gillian spots Barry in the crowd coming down the ramp and there is the long hoped for, tearful reunion. While they're hugging, Roy joins the group of lucky people leaving with the aliens. He's the only one who doesn't get a pair of really cool alien sunglasses that match his jumpsuit, but it's not explained why.

In the end, the ramp closes and as the space ship slowly levitates, preparing to leave, Barry says, "Bye!" from his mother's arms.

I think she has some questions for him.

Sophie's Choice
Playing God

Meryl Streep's portrayal of holocaust survivor Sophie Zawistowski was a once in a lifetime opportunity to showcase her talent. Streep's outstanding portrayal of the tortured Sophie, won her a Golden Globe and Academy Award for Best Actress of 1982.

Relocated to New York from Poland via Auschwitz concentration camp, Sophie is haunted by her experiences during the Second World War. While being brow beat by a churlish librarian, a pale, thin Sophie collapses, convinced she is dying. Nathan Landau (Kevin Kline) comes to her rescue, assures her she isn't dying, just in need of care. Nathan takes her to his brother the physician who, according to Sophie, treats her for scurvy, typhus, anemia and scarlet fever.

When Sophie regains her health, she and Nathan become lovers. If Sophie is unaware that Nathan is a diagnosed paranoid-schizophrenic when they meet, it isn't long before she discovers Nathan has some problems of his own. Drinking brings out Nathan's dark side and he likes to drink. Sometimes he doesn't need the booze as a catalyst to get crazy. When he has an episode it is usually accompanied by ugly accusations of Sophie's imaginary unfaithfulness. She accepts Nathan's paranoid outbursts and abuse as part of his illness.

One thing is certain, it's never dull around Nathan.

When a new boarder, Stingo (Peter McNicol), moves in, his upstairs neighbors invite him for dinner that night. Before he can go up, Stingo hears a commotion in the hall and finds Sophie and Nathan in the middle of a bitter fight. When Stingo challenges Nathan's behavior, she is defensive of Nathan, no matter how horrible he treats her or what he says. He is her savior and she clings to him with the desperation of a drowning person clinging to a life preserver. Nothing he does or says can drive her away.

Nathan needs Sophie as much as she needs him. They are both tortured souls trying to survive, looking to each other for support to make it through another day.

Their pain and angst comes from different sources. Sophie can't escape her past and Nathan can't escape his confusion. Sophie doesn't smile without feeling guilty and her smiles are rare, fleeting, and usually alcohol induced.

Her story emerges as she slowly opens up to Stingo. At first, she can only bear to tell him a portion of the events that shaped her current life. In spite of her confinement to a concentration camp, Sophie is a Polish Catholic, her father and husband are noted and vocal Polish anti-Semitics. Her husband is a disciple of her father, a noted Polish jurist. In spite of her father and husband's activities on behalf of the Nazis, they are executed along with the rest of the Polish intelligentsia during the German occupation of Poland.

Sophie is left with her two young children, Jan and Eva, in an increasingly hostile world. Approached by the Polish underground to translate stolen German documents, she refuses. When she's asked why she won't help, she replies, "I can't. I can't endanger my children."

Wanda, her friend in the resistance replies, "Your children could be next."

Not long after, Wanda and her brother, Sophie's lover, are executed by the Gestapo and she herself is arrested. Her protestations that she is a Nazi sympathizer get her nowhere with her interrogators and they process her into their gruesome killing machine, Auschwitz. Sophie's only crime was knowing the wrong people.

It isn't long before Sophie and her children are on a train to Auschwitz. Her young daughter plays a flute and squirms on her lap while her son, only slightly older, looks frightened in the darkened railroad car. No one talks, no one even dare speculate where the train is headed.

In their hearts, they all know.

When they reach their destination, a Nazi officer walks down the line selecting who will live and who will die. When he reaches Sophie, she implores him to spare her children. She speaks to him in perfect upper-class German and protests that she and her children are Catholics and there has been a terrible mistake.

The Nazi officer examines her and her children and notes that they look German. He is attracted to her and considers what sex would be like with her. He tells her to chose between her children and when she protests, he exclaims they can both die as far as he's concerned. In a snap decision, she holds out her daughter who begins to scream when a guard takes her from Sophie's hands. She watches as the guard takes the hysterical girl into the night and the certainty of the gas chamber and ovens.

Her son is taken from her and placed in a separate camp for children. Sophie's knowledge of German and secretarial skills get her a job working as Camp Commandant Hoess' secretary. He makes an awkward pass at her and she uses the opportunity to try and save her son.

Sophie had heard of the typhus epidemic in the children's camp and is terrified for her son, Jan. She goes to her knees and begs that he be included in a Nazi adoption program for Aryan looking children. Hoess reluctantly agrees to move her son into the program to placate her but reneges the next morning and Jan is lost, his fate unknown.

In spite of her best efforts to save the lives of her children, she has failed.

In the end, Sophie and Nathan commit suicide by taking cyanide, lying down on the bed together and dying in each other's arms. They left a world that neither could cope with any longer for entirely different reasons. Sophie clung to Nathan, but he no longer had the strength to help her as he sank further and further into madness.

Sophie Zawistowski was forced to make a decision no mother should have to make. In the end, her decision made no difference and she lost both of her children. In spite of a world gone mad, Sophie could never escape the guilt of her decision or the ultimate horror of having made the choice.

There was no happy ending for Sophie, only tears.

Afterword

I'd like to acknowledge all the great mothers who brought us into the world. Like everything else in life, mothers are all different. Some are exemplary, others are deplorable. Most fall in between.

Being a mother is a tough job and it never really ends. A mother is a mother until the end of her days.

So here's to all you Mom's including my own. Hope you enjoy your special day.

Happy Mother's Day!